P9-AOJ-315

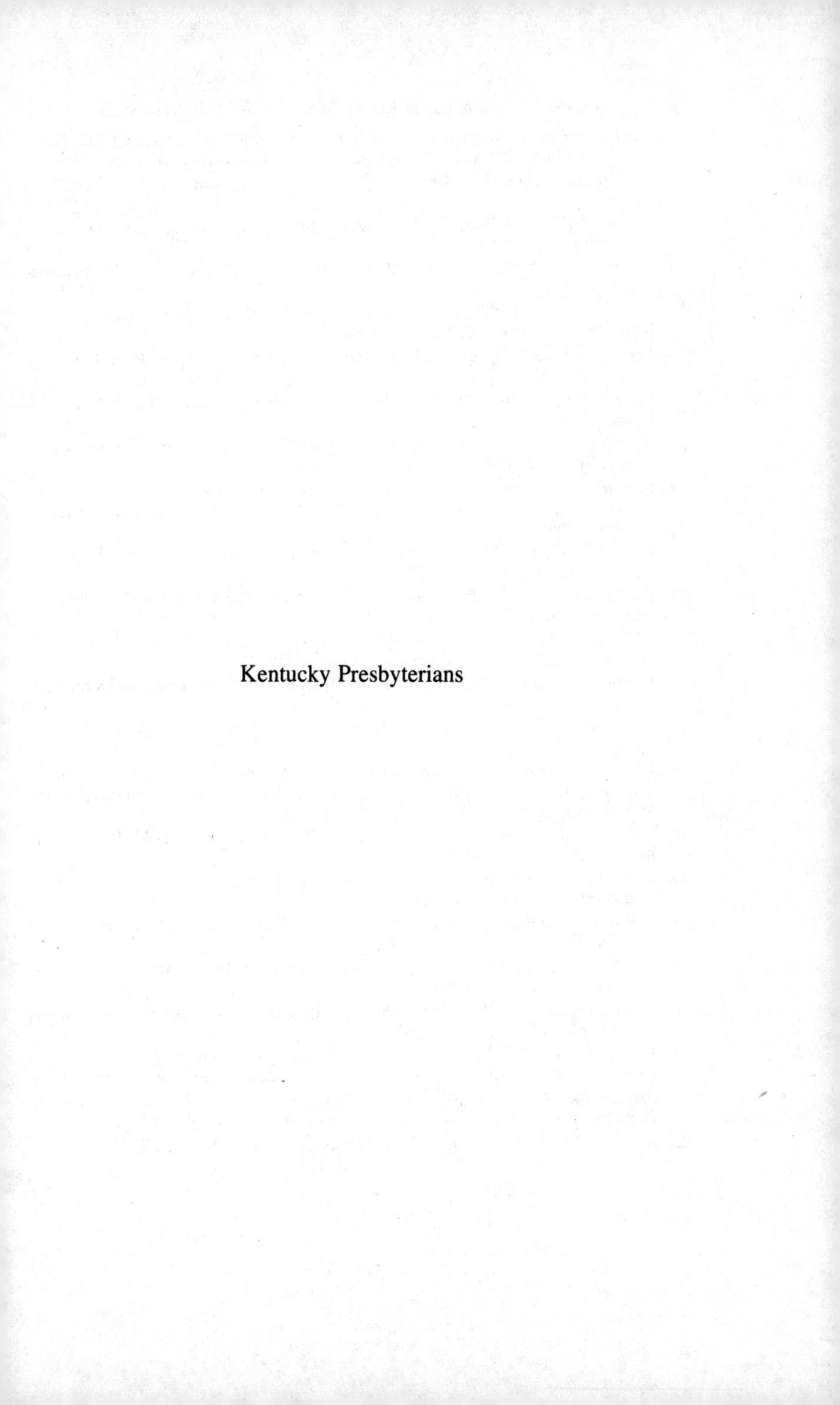

Kentucky Presbyterians

PRESBYTERIAN HISTORICAL SOCIETY PUBLICATIONS

1. *The Presbyterian Enterprise* by M. W. Armstrong, L.A. Loetscher and C.A. Anderson (Westminster Press, 1956; Paperback reprinted for P.H.S., 1963 & 1976)
*2. *Presbyterian Ministry in American Culture* by E. A. Smith (Westminster Press, 1962)
3. *Journals of Charles Beatty, 1762-1769,* edited by Guy S. Klett (Pennsylvania State University Press, 1962)
*4. *Hoosier Zion, The Presbyterian in Early Indiana* by L. C. Rudolph (Yale University Press, 1963)
*5. *Presbyterianism in New York State* by Robert Hastings Nichols, edited and completed by James Hastings Nichols (Westminster Press, 1963)
6. *Scots Breed and Susquehanna* by Hubertis M. Cummings (University of Pittsburgh Press, 1964)
7. *Presbyterians and the Negro—A History* by Andrew E. Murray (Presbyterian Historical Society, 1966)
8. *A Bibliography of American Presbyterianism During the Colonial Period* by Leonard J. Trinterud (Presbyterian Historical Society, 1968)
9. *George Bourne and "The Book and Slavery Irreconcilable"* by John W. Christie and Dwight L. Dumond (Historical Society of Delaware and Presbyterian Historical Society, 1969)
10. *The Skyline Synod: Presbyterianism in Colorado and Utah* by Andrew E. Murray (Synod of Colorado/Utah, 1977)
11. *The Life and Writings of Francis Makemie,* edited by Boyd S. Schlenther (Presbyterian Historical Society, 1971)
12. *A Younger Church in Search of Maturity: Presbyterianism in Brazil from 1910 to 1959* by Paul Pierson (Trinity University Press, 1974)
*13. *Presbyterians in the South,* Vols. II and III, by Ernest Trice Thompson (John Knox Press, 1973)
14. *Ecumenical Testimony* by John McNeill and James H. Nichols (Westminster Press, 1974)
15. *Iglesia Presbiteriana: A History of Presbyterians and Mexican Americans in the Southwest* by R. Douglas Brackenridge and Francisco O. Garcia-Treto (Trinity University Press, 1974)
16. *The Rise and Decline of Education for Black Presbyterians* by Inez M. Parker (Trinity University Press, 1977)
17. *Minutes of the Presbyterian Church in America, 1706-1788* edited by Guy S. Klett (Presbyterian Historical Society, 1977)
18. *Eugene Carson Blake, Prophet with Portfolio* by R. Douglas Brackenridge (Seabury Press, 1978)
19. *Prisoners of Hope: A Search for Mission 1815-1822* by Marjorie Barnhart (Presbyterian Historical Society, 1980)
20. *From Colonalism to World Community: The Church's Pilgrimage* by John Coventry Smith (Geneva Press, 1982)
21. *Facing the Enlightenment and Pietism: Archibald Alexander and the Founding of Princeton Theological Seminary* by Lefferts A. Loetscher (Greenwood Press, 1983)
22. *Presbyterian Women in America: Two Centuries of a Quest for Status* by Lois A. Boyd and R. Douglas Brackenridge (Greenwood Press, 1983)
23. *Kentucky Presbyterians* by Louis B. Weeks (John Knox Press, 1983)

*Out of print.

Kentucky Presbyterians

LOUIS B. WEEKS

John Knox Press
ATLANTA

Library of Congress Cataloging in Publication Data
Weeks, Louis, 1941–
Kentucky Presbyterians.

Includes bibliographical references and index.
1. Presbyterian Church—Kentucky. 2. Kentucky—Church history. I. Title.
BX8947.K4W43 1983 285′.1769 83-8372
ISBN 0-8042-0920-0

10 9 8 7 6 5 4 3 2 1
Printed in the United States of America
John Knox Press
Atlanta, Georgia 30365

To colleagues at the Louisville Presbyterian Seminary—
students, faculty, staff, and other friends in
that part of the Kentucky Presbyterian family.

Preface and Acknowledgments

Not long after I began teaching at Louisville, during the winter of 1970–71, I mentioned to L. C. Rudolph, my predecessor, that Kentucky Presbyterians held a fascination for me. Rudolph had already written *Hoosier Zion* on the early Reformed Christians in Indiana, and I knew he was an expert on the Kentucky area as well. Rudolph politely responded to my casual comment and our conversation turned to other matters. Imagine my surprise when, in the spring of 1971, I received a large file of materials and several boxes of books from him, most of them concerned with Kentucky Presbyterian history.

I like to think that Rudolph walked a little more easily that day, because I suddenly felt the weight of a task—to learn and interpret that history. Initial study of the files showed several people before me had shared enthusiasm for the topic. I remember particularly the correspondence among Rudolph, Robert Stuart Sanders, and Frank Taylor in the late 1950s. Sanders had encouraged Taylor, if memory serves me well, to pick off little chunks of the history before undertaking a more thorough history. "The whole history will be too much to handle . . . R.S.S.," I noted in my files.

My early endeavors, one particularly with James Hickey, an elder at the Crescent Hill Presbyterian Church and a lawyer, focused on the lawsuits and battles in Kentucky Presbyterian history. There were many! If Rudolph wrote *Hoosier Zion*, I would have to relate "Bluegrass Armageddon." More recently, however, my specific studies have concentrated on Terah Templin, Stuart Robinson, John G. Fee, and others whose fighting took a back seat to more constructive enterprises. I have grown increasingly respectful of E. O. Guerrant, whose distinctive contributions I will continue to explore.

A request from Dr. Glenn Dorris and Mr. Charles Castner of Second Presbyterian Church, Louisville, to write a sesquicentennial history of that congregation provided a providential case study in preparation for the broader topic. Interest from students at the seminary in the early revival led me to work on the sacramental occasions as one source of the phenomenon.

Kentucky Presbyterian history even now holds a fascination for me, eleven years after I began to study it in detail. The interaction of Presbyterians, Methodists, Catholics, and Baptists in this distinctive environment certainly will claim my attention in the future. The special stories of the Cumberland Presbyterian Church, the Associate Reformed Presbyterian Church, and the other Reformed communions deserve more attention than they here receive. And the subsequent histories of the Christian Church (Disciples of Christ) and the Shaker communities, after Presbyterians helped to form them in this area, remain subjects of value in research.

The Louisville Presbyterian Seminary under presidents Albert C. Winn and C. Ellis Nelson graciously supported my long-term study of the persons and institutions in our local history. The current president, John M. Mulder, has read critically the entire manuscript, and he has led the quest for subsidies to enable publication. Deans Clinton Morrison and Grayson Tucker allowed me to be released from certain teaching responsibilities in order to pursue the subject.

Cooperative Presbyterians and other helpful colleagues in history have assisted in the gathering of materials. I must mention just a few who gave particular assistance. Mr. and Mrs. William Donan, Mrs. Olive Eldred, the Rev. Ed Wicklein, Dr. Thomas Spragens, Mrs. Anita Green, Mr. Van Norman, Miss Mary Cleland Adams, Miss Caroline Grimes, the Rev. Charles Hanna, the Rev. Mary Morgan, the Rev. William Peterson, Dr. Clyde Crews, and many others have gone far beyond the performance of duties to be of really valuable assistance.

The directors and staffs of the Presbyterian Historical Society, the Presbyterian Historical Foundation, the Kentucky Historical Society, the Filson Club, and several other institutions have cooperated thoroughly with my requests for information and materials. The reference librarians of the University of Louisville, the Louisville Free Public Library, the Southern Baptist Theological Seminary, Centre, Pikeville, and Berea colleges have also proven to be extremely courteous and "resourceful." Mr. Ernest White, Mrs. Sharon Paul, Miss Delia Collins, and many more folk at the Louisville Presbyterian Theological Seminary library have cheerfully made room for the historian-as-eccentric, and they have persistently collected a fine library of immense usefulness. Mr. Stephen Hamilton Wright worked with me in final editing and authentication of notes. Mrs. Gloria Bryant, Mrs. Jean Knipp, and Mrs. Norma Porterfield all served cheerfully to make the various drafts into legible typescripts.

My own family cooperated throughout the period of research and writing. Dr. Carolyn Weeks, Lou Weeks, and Sid Weeks read portions of the manuscript critically, and Mrs. Doretta Mang and Mrs. Mary Weeks provided proofreading skills for the project. Errors and shortcomings, of course, remain my personal responsibility.

Louis Weeks
Louisville Presbyterian Seminary

Contents

INTRODUCTION

The Structure of Kentucky Presbyterianism

The Presbyterians came early to Kentucky, and members of the Reformed denominations have exercised a profound influence on the life of the commonwealth throughout its history. Movements and institutions spawned among the Presbyterians have exerted an even more thorough impact upon the state. The story of their coming and development deserves attention. The quarrels and unions they had, the personalities of their leaders, and the life in their congregations are all subjects of intrinsic value.

This study is the first in a number of years to give attention to institutions and individuals throughout Kentucky Presbyterian history.[1] During the nineteenth century several denominational histories provided excellent accounts of Reformed life, and a number of general histories noted contributions of Presbyterians to the common welfare.[2] More recently, state histories have frequently ignored religion or merely dismissed its impact with some passing characterizations.[3] But in none of the United States has religious life in general, Presbyterian life in particular, had greater bearing upon continuing social institutions and familial patterns than in Kentucky. And no study of Kentucky Presbyterians offers a comprehensible structure for the interpretation of their history.

The complex relationships and diversity of interests among Kentucky Presbyterians seemingly would preclude any schema that at once remained true to the facts and provided insight into the nature of the denomination(s). If Presbyterians eschewed revivals, for example, they also employed revivals throughout most of their history. If they embodied drives for temperance and Sabbatarianism, they also included distillers and employers of Sunday laborers among their number; many Presbyterians also worked on Sunday. If hosts of Kentucky Shakers and Christians (Disciples of Christ) came from the Presbyterians, many others joined Reformed communions from Baptist or Catholic backgrounds. Thus the Presbyterians in Kentucky would apparently defy classification.

On the other hand, the nature of Presbyterianism in the commonwealth has changed through the years. In its early decades, the church and its institutions struggled merely to survive. Hostilities arose in setting the direction of the church. Soon afterward, bitter fights characterized the church. Regional loyalties replaced a sense of national purpose as a primary value for most Presbyterians. After the Civil War, the churches moved in a gentle but parochial manner to seek evangelization in all portions of the state and to heal fractures from previous internecine strife. Finally, in the twentieth century, congregations and judicatories have become increasingly ecumenical in both attitudes and actions.

More general histories of American religion might point along similar developmental lines—from a tenuous existence, to a divided and contested one, to honoring a degree of consensus, to sharing power and leadership with others. More theological studies could focus on the differing emphases in various aspects of the articulated belief structure. Presbyterians, for example, early emphasized atonemental doctrine with affirmation or questioning of penal substitutionary statements of it. They moved to center upon its sacrificial aspects, then its vicarious nature, and most recently upon Christ as transcending special theories of atonement.

This mix of institutional and social history of the Presbyterians must remain more modest in its scope. Though neat "periods" of history do not clearly mark the history, the Presbyterians did move from being a frontier church, almost a sect in discipline and self-identification, to becoming a deeply divided border church by at least 1835. By 1883, mutual disparagement had largely ceased, and Presbyterians had become generally more tolerant of one another, more interested in evangelism. They began to send persons and goods to less cosmopolitan areas of the state, to other "home missions" fields, and to other lands.

Thus Presbyterians had moved toward sharing the faith at a time when many of America's religious bodies still fought over creeds, doctrines, and institutions. This new religious climate deserves the title "heartland Presbyterianism," for the term indicates both the center of piety in emotions and feelings, and its centrism in social and religious doctrine.

Well into the twentieth century Presbyterianism lost its sense of competition with other religious bodies, or at least most of the interest focused upon cooperation and ecumenical activity. Presbyterians helped to found and staff many of the ecumenical bodies in the state of Kentucky (as in other portions of the country). This ecumenical period continues today.

PART I.
Frontier

The Rev. James Blythe (1765–1842), early pastor of the Clear Creek and Pisgah Churches, Woodford County.

Typical early church building. This is the Upper Benson Church, 1795, the first in Franklin County.

CHAPTER 1.

Beginnings

In 1847, historian Robert Davidson began his history of the Presbyterians in Kentucky by speaking first of the settlement of the Valley of Virginia by the Scotch-Irish. He told of colonial congregations and then recounted some of the stories of early explorers. Davidson paid special attention to the McAfee party because, as he contended, they had such an "intimate connection with the planting of the Church."[1] Davidson perceived Presbyterian movement into Kentucky as an extension of the Reformed presence from a more settled environment.

Many facts suggest the validity of this interpretation of Presbyterian beginnings in the area. The importance of the Scotch-Irish cannot be denied; movement did come first from Virginia's "West" when numbers of settlers arrived, and the McAfees represented a pious presence in all its dimensions. Missionaries and money came from Hanover Presbytery in Virginia, and the interaction between Kentucky and Virginia frequently resembled that of an extended family or clan.

The Scotch-Irish received their ethnic designation from blood and location. Scots had been encouraged to settle in northern Ireland under James I in 1610, as a British plan to help pacify the island. Thousands had migrated to the counties of the Ulster Plantation, proving as obstreperous for the rulers as those they had replaced. At the same time, the Scotch-Irish experienced continual pressures to maintain their ethnic identity and their religious vitality for more than a century. As persecution increased while crops failed periodically during the eighteenth century, massive numbers of the people immigrated to the American colonies. The majority of these Irish citizens of Scot descent professed a Reformed theology and a Presbyterian form of government for the church.[2]

First Settlers

Many of the Scotch-Irish took advantage of the comparative freedom they found in Maryland and Pennsylvania to settle there, but others leap-frogged the civilized seaboard in Virginia and the Carolinas to populate the more isolated places to the west of the towns. So many established farms and villages along the rivers such as Cape Fear, Shenandoah, and Rappahanock that the areas became known as ''Presbyterian valleys.''[3] From there branches of the families again moved westward to occupy other river valleys—the Yadkin, the Kanawha, and the Monongahela. Still others moved southward from Pennsylvania to join fresh waves of immigrants. Davidson described them by clans, as he recounted the Presbyterian settlement of the Blue Ridge:

> Besides the McDowells and Alexanders, may be mentioned the families of the Pattons, the Moores, the Telfords, the Matthewes, the Prestons, the Paxtons, the Lyles, the Stuarts, the Crawfords, the Cumminses, the Browns, the Wallaces, the Wilsons, the Carutherses, the Campbells, the McCampbells, the McClungs, the McCues, the McKees, the McCouns, etc.[4]

The McAfee party was one of the significant groups to explore Kentucky, and its members constituted one of the first settlements. According to most accounts, James, George, and Robert McAfee, James McCoun, Sr., and Samuel Adams comprised the party of 1773. They encountered and coordinated their exploration with surveyor Hancock Taylor's party, and with larger parties under Thomas Bullitt and James Harrod.[5] It was during this summer, after the separation of the McAfee group from the rest, that Robert McAfee perceived a work of ''Providence,'' and the account provided a glimpse into the Presbyterian perspective on divine care:

> They had reached the highest point of land in the west and altho in

> sight of the promised land, they were literally starving as they had been without a mouthful to eat for two days. Their feet were blistered and their legs and thighs raw. . . . All day long no change for the better presented itself. The sun was beginning to descend. . . . George McAfee and Samuel Adams, exhausted by fatigue, hunger and despair threw themselves on the ground and declared that they could proceed no further. . . . At length Robert McAfee as a last effort of despair determined . . . to see if he could find anything to kill. . . . The sun was by this time with its last setting beams, gilding the highest points of the adjacent mountains, when that almighty hand, which guides, and directs the affairs of this world, interposed on their behalf. . . . He saw a small spike buck, about fifty yards from him. Joy, anxiety, and desperation all flashed on his mind at once, but being an excellent marksman, he fired and the buck fell. . . .[6]

The McAfees returned to Virginia for the winter, but hostilities on the frontier throughout 1774 prevented their spending time in Kentucky during that year. On 11 March, 1775, they occupied land they had claimed earlier, and they quarreled with James Harrod who had managed to avoid the violence long enough during the previous year to erect some cabins nearby. The McAfee party moved a portion of their claims and constructed a "Station" which in times of stress became a companion fort adjacent to Harrod's Station. The party of 1775 also included William McAfee, John Higgins and Sever Poulson (who were evidently servants) with David Adams, brother of Samuel, as well as Samuel and George McGee.[7] They actively sought formation of Presbyterian churches, and most of their number served as leaders in the "New Providence" Church, located near the place where the deer fell.[8]

Granted the simplicity of the thesis that Scotch-Irish from Virginia gave Kentucky its Presbyterian presence, a broader perspective yields a more accurate interpretation of the matter. By the time people with a Reformed heritage moved into Kentucky, English and Scotch-Irish Presbyterians had together formed a distinctly American tradition.[9] Many of the settlers possessed French and Dutch backgrounds as well, and they came from Pennsylvania, North Carolina, and a host of other locations to Kentucky. Thus while many of the first leaders were Scotch-Irish from Virginia's Valley, it is an over-generalization to claim that Kentucky's earliest settlers were homogeneous or came from one location.

Descriptions of early Kentucky Presbyterians need to include the slaves, Afro-Americans who accompanied their owners westward. While few blacks could participate actively in church affairs, and fewer still were allowed to take any positions of responsibility, many blacks attended the first congregational gatherings and belonged to the churches. Frequently their labor built the buildings and maintained them, whether or not they could attend worship.[10]

Many of Kentucky's first settlers, from a variety of backgrounds and with varying degrees of commitment, helped to lead congregations in forming Presbyterianism in the commonwealth. A few of the most significant should be noted, if only in brief fashion. Caleb Wallace, Benjamin Logan, Samuel McDowell, Jane Stevenson, and Jacob Fishback were just five of them.

Caleb Wallace, certainly one of the most colorful and influential of the early Presbyterian settlers, had moved from ministry into law by the time he entered Kentucky in late 1782.[11] Wallace had grown up in the Valley of Virginia, but he had journeyed north to the College of New Jersey for theological education. He returned to pastor the Cub Creek and Little Falling River Churches in Augusta County. Wallace and his family were deeply tied to Kentucky's settlement, because he and his wife, Rosanna Christian, owned property in the "West," as did several other members of her family. Colonel William Fleming, one brother-in-law, held at least 20,000 acres in central and western Kentucky. Gradually Wallace moved toward jurisprudence and away from the pastoral ministry. He was appointed to the Commission for the Adjudication of Western Accounts. Caleb Wallace, Rosanna, and their family, together with Wallace's brother Andrew, his father Samuel, and a brother-in-law Colonel Henry Prawling and all their households made the move to the Bluegrass in 1782. Already wealthy, Wallace became more affluent as he acquired land and slaves. He helped argue myriad lawsuits over disputed boundaries and began serving on the Kentucky Court of Appeals in 1792. He helped to secure statehood for Kentucky, and he fostered the founding of Transylvania Seminary, the first of the state's educational institutions. He still found time to teach apprentice lawyers, some of the first who were trained locally, and to assist in the establishment of Presbyterian Church courts at the presbytery and synod level.[12]

Samuel McDowell, born in Pennsylvania in 1735, was reared in

Virginia and served in colonial regiments during a number of major engagements with the Indians—at Braddock's defeat, for example, and in Dunmore's War. Rewarded for his services with western lands, McDowell moved to Kentucky only after he had led a Revolutionary regiment against the British. He was appointed Surveyor of Public Lands in Fayette, which included all central Kentucky at the time, and he located his family and office in the area in 1783. McDowell's leadership in the constitutional conventions was instrumental in bringing Kentucky into the Union. He also gave leadership to, and helped pay for the establishment of the Presbyterian Church in Danville. He and his wife Mary McClung produced several children who likewise proved extremely important as Kentucky leaders—Joseph McDowell, an elder in the Danville church; William McDowell who helped begin a congregation in Bowling Green; and Dr. Ephriam McDowell who helped lead first Transylvania University and then Centre College under the Presbyterians, although he became an Episcopalian.[13]

Jane Gay Stevenson, who lived much of her life in Kentucky frontier Presbyterianism, was among the few women whose remembrances received attention by historians. She moved from Augusta County, Virginia, in 1780, to the Bluegrass area where Lexington later developed. She and her husband Samuel found frontier life similar to life in the Valley of Virginia before they migrated. She remembered that even on the road to enter Kentucky, the family refrained from Sunday travel because of the prohibition of the Fourth Commandment against work on the Sabbath. Thus her family brought an applied faith as they settled, before public worship became formalized.[14]

Jacob Fishback came to Kentucky before he became Presbyterian, probably in 1784. He farmed quietly and he speculated on land purchases. He moved several times and helped several Presbyterian congregations. At his death, members of Fishback's family discovered a number of private prayers which he had written as an exercise in piety. The prayers exhibited a Reformed theology that could be termed "representative" of Presbyterian laypeople—ascriptions to God as triune, petitions for sanctification, and a large measure of the language of praise:

> To thee I solemnly and deliberately dedicate myself, my soul and body; my soul, with all its powers of understanding, will and affections; my body, and all its members and senses; my time and talents,

> my whole family, children and servants; I give up to thee all my estate, all that I am and all that I have or possess. Amen, and Amen. Let All the Angels of Heaven say amen. A-m-e-n, O my soul.[15]

Fishbacks and Stevensons, Logans, McAfees, and Wallaces were just five of the families that together settled the area. They and hundreds of other clan-like families made quick work of the business of carving homes on the frontier.

Many Kentuckians had been baptized Presbyterians, but no longer participated in the life of a particular congregation. Benjamin Logan, who migrated early to erect his own "St. Asaph's Station" and who contributed to the process of obtaining statehood, offers one example. He had been baptized as an infant by the Rev. John Craig in Virginia. In Kentucky, Logan read the Bible and helped his children learn the catechism. Though his wife Ann was a stalwart member of the church, Benjamin Logan evidently remained unaffiliated.[16]

In addition to the other settlers, a number of Presbyterian ministers moved quickly into Kentucky. A word about first pastors helps supplement information about the settlers.

First Pastors

The first historian of Kentucky, John Filson, in his *Discovery, Settlement and Present State of Kentucky* (1784) proclaimed "the Rev. David Rice, of Virginia" the first pastor of the Presbyterians in the area.[17] Robert Bishop's *Outline of the History of the Church in the State of Kentucky* so accentuated Rice's contribution that all other early pastors seemed insignificant by comparison.[18] Finally, when Davidson presented Rice as almost singlehandedly starting the early congregations, the place of David Rice was secure.[19] Major histories, almost without exception, name Rice as the "first" Presbyterian minister who "gathered the scattered membership of this church into three congregations."[20]

Actually, history indicates that four men vie for the honor, and each was "first pastor" for Presbyterians in Kentucky—Terah Templin, James Mitchel, Caleb Wallace, and Rice. A fifth, Adam Rankin, was the first called to Kentucky as pastor of a particular church. Each of the five deserves attention as a pioneer, for each contributed to the growth of the Reformed church family in Kentucky.[21]

Templin was the first preacher, and he arrived in 1780. He preached several times that summer as a licentiate of Hanover Presbytery. He probably came back during 1781, and when his father, John, moved to Danville from Bedford County, Virginia, Terah Templin doubtlessly accompanied him. Terah, born in 1742, had studied for the ministry after the death of his fiancée.[22] At Liberty Hall, Templin had received support from Robert Carter, III, a wealthy landowner and Baptist lay leader.[23] Licensed to preach in 1780, he immediately went to Kentucky as a missionary.

When he received a formal call to a particular ministry Templin also received final ordination—in 1785. His first responsibilities were to supply "vacant churches in Jefferson and Nelson Counties."[24] He preached at various times in established congregations; the Presbyterian church in Lebanon credits him with organizing that congregation in 1794.

When Presbyterians moved west to Livingston County, Templin moved with the family of John Caldwell in 1799 to open churches in the western area of the state. He remained a bachelor, and he evidently did not take money for his services.[25]

A Baptist scholar, William Whitsett, argued forcefully that James Mitchel was the first Presbyterian minister in Kentucky. As a licentiate of Hanover Presbytery, Mitchel, in 1781 began to gather various families of Presbyterians for worship in a regular fashion, making pastoral calls as well as preaching. His work at Concord (Danville), Cane Run (Harrodsburg), and at the Fork of Dix (Dicks) River culminated in the request in May, 1783, by people in that area for the presence of David Rice to lead their emergent congregations.[26]

Born in Piqua, Pennsylvania, January 29, 1747, James Mitchel had moved with his family to Cub Creek in Charlotte County, Virginia, where he became a communicant of the Presbyterian Church in 1764. He had served as a tutor at Hampden Sydney College, perhaps as he followed theological studies there. Licensed in 1781, Mitchel, according to Whitsett, worked in Kentucky and perceived its promise. He returned to Virginia praising the area and migrated again after taking a bride in Virginia.

Mitchel returned another time to Bedford, Virginia, for ordination, and in 1784 journeyed back to Danville to become the first teacher for the newly-instituted Transylvania Seminary. After a year in Kentucky, he moved back again to pastor the congregation at Peaks of Otter in Virginia.[27]

The third man, Caleb Wallace, could be described as the "first, permanent, ordained Presbyterian minister in Kentucky." Wallace certainly had received ordination, and he arrived to stay in Kentucky in 1782. Five years older than Mitchel and probably his good friend, Wallace had been pastor of the Cub Creek Church while Mitchel belonged. Wallace presumably moved from ministry into law when his first wife died and he married for a second time. But he did not demit the ministry, and he did lead a funeral service, as well as regular Lord's Day worship in his new home.[28]

David Rice, usually granted premier place, visited Kentucky in 1783 at the urging of Mitchel. Templin and Wallace already resided in the area through which Rice passed. His avowed intent "to procure settlements for some of his numerous family" resulted in disappointment and frustration on Rice's sojourn.[29]

While in Kentucky, Rice, the preacher, preached for incipient congregations in the Bluegrass. When he returned to Virginia, he received a written request from three hundred potential members to move permanently to Kentucky and to minister among them. Rice obtained permission from Hanover Presbytery, and he located his family in Danville in October, 1783.[30]

Whatever his numerical rank in arrival, David Rice was the "Father" of Reformed Christianity in Kentucky. The accuracy of that designation cannot be disputed. He arrived as the first ordained and practicing member of the clergy. Rice already had received the informal title, "Father," in Virginia.[31] Kentucky Presbyterians regularly addressed him as "Father Rice," with good reason. It was he who had convinced Templin to undertake theological education, and his daughter, Frances B. Rice, was the wife of Mitchel. His move to Kentucky coalesced relationships between McAfees and Wallaces, McDowells and Caldwells, and in fact, many of the early families in the area.[32]

Rice himself had come from a farming family in Hanover County, Virginia, which had been devoted to the Church of England. A sermon by the Presbyterian dissenter, Samuel Davies, provided the occasion for Rice to resolve a longstanding personal religious struggle.[33] As a young man Rice had converted to Presbyterianism in the mid-1750s, and he subsequently read theology with the Reverend John Todd. When Davies became president of the College of New Jersey, Rice enrolled there and was graduated in 1761.[34] He returned to Virginia and received licensure from Hanover Presbytery. Rice married Mary Blair, daughter of Samuel Blair (who had taught Davies). Ordained in 1763 to succeed Davies in Hanover churches, Rice experienced contentiousness there and moved to the Peaks of Otter Church in 1769.[35]

Once in Kentucky, Rice did oversee the organization of the three congregations that formed a center for pioneer Kentucky Presbyterianism. He likewise promoted the beginnings of Transylvania Seminary, where his son-in-law came to teach. He oversaw the formation of Transylvania Presbytery, and he agitated against the institution of slavery. Evidently Rice became increasingly bitter as time went by, and he retired with a portion of his family to Green County in 1798, thereafter preaching only in supply positions until his death in 1816.[36]

Meanwhile, during 1784 another Presbyterian minister, Adam Rankin, arrived in the neighborhood of Jane Stevenson and her family near Lexington. Rankin, from Pennsylvania, had attended Liberty Hall and had been licensed by Hanover Presbytery. He had ties to the other ministers, both from having served churches in Augusta County, Virginia, and in having married a woman from there—Martha, the daughter of Alexander McPheeters. Rankin helped organize the Mt. Zion Church in Lexington, and he served for a while the (New) Pisgah Church, which arose outside of that community.[37]

Other ministers did come at approximately the same time—for instance, Andrew McClure, who helped organize the Salem Church, visited Kentucky in 1784 and returned the following year to settle permanently. James Crawford bought some land and moved his family to the Walnut Hill neighborhood six miles from Lexington. Crawford served that congregation as it grew, first as a licentiate and then as an ordained minister.[38]

Pioneer Life

The earliest explorers, the initial settlers, and the larger numbers of those who followed soon afterward—all experienced radically different living conditions in Kentucky. The explorers and surveying parties simply wanted to chart what they found and get what they could. Some lived according to a rather rigid code of ethics and followed religious scruples. Others did not suffer from an overactive conscience, to put the matter mildly.[39]

It could be argued that religious aversion to violence prevented many of the faithful, Presbyterians and others, from crossing the Cumberland Gap, moving down from Western Pennsylvania, or otherwise entering the area to find furs, land, or minerals. To enter the "Cain-Tuck" meant confronting in hostile fashion the Indian tribes of Shawnee, Wyandot, and Miami, and a distinct possibility of "kill or be killed." If so, then a process of self-selection occurred among the more bellicose and less stable elements in colonial America. By the same token, people who moved to Kentucky possessed self-confidence and the ability to tolerate the ambiguities and hardships of pioneer life. Too, it may have been that the comparative wealth of professing Reformed Protestants sapped their willingness to "pull up stakes" and to venture into an unknown territory. Whatever the reasons, and all of these stated can be supported with evidence, the fact remains that few of the explorers and first settlers gave a high priority to religious observance.[40]

The first settlers, many of whom had previously sojourned in the land, sought simply to survive and perchance to thrive economically. Glowing reports of the fertility of the soil, the plentiful supply of game, and the availability of cheap land had lured them in the first place. Yet not all was as promoted. Henderson had been advertising the land as though he owned it as early as December 1774. Surveys by early parties not equipped for accurate charting of new territory, and competing legal systems in early days, compounded difficulties in obtaining clear titles to land. McClung, as a lawyer and an early historian, located the chief source of confusion in the land law of Virginia providing for piece-meal, owner-sponsored surveying of western lands. "Unnumbered sorrows, lawsuits, and heart-rending vexations, were the consequence," he concluded.[41] When Rice first came to look over the situation, he decided against entering the legal fray: "I saw that the spirit of speculation was flowing in such a torrent that it would bear down every weak obstacle. . . . I knew the make of my own mind, that I could not enjoy the happiness of life if engaged in disputes and lawsuits. I therefore resolved to return home without securing a single foot of land.''[42]

The routine of daily life proved difficult for early Kentuckians, even for the more affluent of the pioneers. Log cabins with dirt floors and mud chimneys were the first ''permanent'' dwellings. Larger cabins with brick or stone fireplaces became typical homes in the 1780s. But even in the 1790s when clapboard and brick homes of the well-to-do began to appear, the winters proved hard to endure and the land remained difficult to work by hand. Furniture was rough-hewn with few exceptions; utensils were mostly wooden and homemade, too. Salt came from wells at ''licks'' after a lengthy reduction process; sugar came from maples and an even more time-consuming method of drying the sap to a solid (or settling for a syrup). Corn was hand-ground in most places until well into the 1780s. Clothes came almost exclusively from hand-fashioned wool, skins, or hemp products. The list of everyday, survival tasks seemed endless and most families had to do all of them. For the few slaves the work was usually the least desirable and the rewards most meager.[43]

The most intense threat to life came from the violent relationships with Indians. ''Raiding parties'' were constant between Indians and settlers. The lines between warfare and lawlessness, seldom distinct, remained blurred indeed on the Kentucky frontier. Settlers and Indians were killed, wounded and captured, as battles raged periodically. George Rogers Clark, for one, fought almost constantly in either planning or executing attacks from March, 1777, when he began serving as the ranking militia officer, until September, 1783, when the Treaty of Paris was signed.[44] He and his occasional army ranged up and down the Ohio in various engagements. The ''Indian menace'' continued until Anthony Wayne was victorious at Fallen Timbers in 1794.[45]

Tales of atrocities by the Indians evidently provided much of the frontier fodder for conversation. Many accounts were true, gruesome, and scary. ''Joseph McCoun, a promising lad, the youngest and darling son of his father, and the favorite of the whole family, was surprised and captured by a party of Shawnee, and burned at the stake, on the other side of the Ohio, with excruciating tortures. This event took place in 1781. . . .''[46] Again, historians recounted the bravery of two ''Mrs. Cooks,'' wives of brothers on farms near what is now Frankfort. They held off Wyandot raiding parties that had killed their husbands and now sought to burn them out of their cabin. One woman bit into musket balls to form them with her teeth for her rifle. They fought the flames with the bloody coat of a dead defender. The two women successfully drove off more than a hundred Indians.[47]

These and other tales of murder and scalping, torture and rape, kept early settlers alert to the possibility of Indian attack and its consequences. Perhaps the potential for Indian uprising had more direct bearing on the lives of most settlers than did the actual battles. As congregations formed, they habitually carried long rifles and posted guards when worship occured. All preachers and lay members seemed to have stories of narrow escapes from the Indians (if indeed they had not experienced actual capture). One minister recalled missing a rendezvous with a party for campfire as he traveled; he found them, several dead or wounded, and thanked God he had been spared from the Indian attack. Another Presbyterian remembered people being shot at as they returned home from church in 1790.[48]

Word of the killings and threats to life seemed to suffice as reasons for "retaliation," and numerous Indian villages were completely destroyed in the name of "public safety." In one poignant example, Joseph Ruder is said "to have been out on a creek and seeing an Indian fishing, and a good opportunity to kill, and he thought well if that Indian had as good a chance as I have wouldn't he shoot—yes he would! And accordingly raised his gun and tipped him over on the log, and left him lay. Never went to see him."[49] Most pervasive appears to have been the sense of "ethical justice" as new settlers experienced little sense of responsibility to share either the land or the benefits of European life with the previous inhabitants. Was it not right to destroy the Indian "savages" who threatened life and property? Matching the horror stories about Indians were, as already indicated, tales of courageous Kentucky leaders—Boone, Clark, and Logan among them. Was it not "justice" that such wonderful heroes succeed in taming the wild country and enjoy the fruits of their labors? Kentuckians spent little energy in pondering replies to these questions. They joined in the chorus of affirmations that they would share in the riches of the new land.[50]

Like everyone else, early Kentucky Presbyterians were almost all farmers. As quickly as they could plant a crop, they did so, despite threats of destruction. If they had a measure of wealth, they might hire the work done or purchase people to do it. But more likely, as early pioneers remembered, everyone ploughed and chopped, harvested and stored the food.[51]

Sex roles were rigidly defined in early Kentucky public life, both for Presbyterians and for the general population. "Man's work" consisted in following the various professions and skilled crafts such as "smithing" and "coopering," working the fields on a regular basis, and maintaining equipment. "Woman's work" included all the housework, the manufacture of family needs such as soap and clothes, and "helping out" at harvest and planting times. Although much of the labor appears to have been shared, pioneers who wrote about it seemed to know which jobs were for women and girls, which for boys and men. It is significant that among settlers, men did all the fighting against Indians except in extremely grave situations.[52]

Evidence suggests that sex roles were not so carefully followed in the private lives of persons and families. Daniel Drake, who later reminisced about frontier life in Kentucky before 1800, remembered that as a boy he helped with laundry on washday, with approval of the whole family. He also recalled helping his mother milk their cows, but confessed, "Mother, quite as much as myself, would have been mortified, if any neighboring boy or man had caught me at it."[53]

Word about the rigidity of sex role stereotyping is important in itself, but it also helps to explain the anomaly in which history of the period must be written. For while the majority of members in the early congregations in Kentucky—Presbyterian, as well as the rest—were female, the only leaders of record were men. Except at the actual revivals women could exercise leadership only in informal ways. Thus men's contributions were those recorded, for the most part, and the history involves the naming of almost all men, seldom any women. Wives of ministers and elders frequently are named only as Mrs. __________, providing no Christian names for the women even in Chrisian communities. As records improved during the nineteenth century, notice of women's contributions also increased.

Slavery also appeared very early in Kentucky. Historians have noted that Benjamin Logan brought a slave family, a woman named "Molly" and her three sons, to his little St. Asaph's Station. Other Virginians and settlers from Carolina possessed slaves who accompanied them west. By one account, the "greatest demand" for slaves occurred at the very beginnings of Kentucky settlement, when an immense amount of labor was needed immediately to clear fields, make crops, and build homes. As a social institution, the system of slavery existed as it had in the settled colonies, but the ethics and the value of slavery came under scrutiny quickly in the new land.[54]

Father David Rice published his "Slavery Inconsistent with Justice and Good Policy" in anticipation of the gathering of a constitutional convention in 1792. Rice said that humanity—every person—received the gift of freedom from God. His unequivocal condemnation of the institution of slavery said a "curse" attended slavery, and "national vices will be punished with national calamities." But in the press of achieving social and political organization, Rice's warning went unheeded.[55]

Social organization of Kentucky did occur quickly, and the formation of congregations and Presbyterian judicatories was part of the process. The institutional history supplements the primary social history of frontier Presbyterianism.

CHAPTER 2.

Organization

Presbyterians, recognizing the universality of the church, felt they belonged to Christ's body even when they journeyed away from the tightly-knit congregations in which they had lived. Once they deemed it feasible in the new setting they again established congregations, sessions, connectional courts, and institutions for education. On the frontier, however, even institutions bore a tentative quality that corresponded to the tenuousness of human life itself.

The stories of the people and the institutions together weave the story of the Presbyterian Church on the frontier. In their fluidity and complexity, the institutions sprang up like mushrooms after a rain.

First Congregations and Sessions

The settlers and preachers who came first to the area formed Presbyterian congregations together. On the one hand, congregations came into existence when "heads of families" would petition to call a preacher and promise payment for his services. On the other hand, congregations formed as ministers made itinerations and preached at stated times. Presbyterians, neither established in colonial America nor a "voluntary denomination" in Scotland or Northern Ireland, had a difficult time structurally as they began building a church in a new territory. Perhaps that fact, more than the traditional one of ministerial stability, inhibited the growth of congregations.[1]

Actually, the congregation itself presents something of an anomaly for Presbyterians. For Baptists the congregation is the church, but for connectional Presbyterians the congregation possesses very limited meaning and authority. The greater power for Presbyterians lies in church courts, representative bodies that include the session, presbytery, synod, and assembly. Thus, while congregations remained extremely important in religious formation and identification, they did not receive the same attention that other denominations gave them.[2]

When Rice came to Kentucky, and when Templin, Mitchel, and he preached, Presbyterians did respond by asking that they be formed into congregations and that Rice and others minister for them. In 1783, Rice "organized and took charge of" the first three congregations of Presbyterians in Kentucky: Concord at Danville; Cane Run at Trigg's Station; and the Fork of Dicks (Dix) River.[3] Some partisan historians would designate one or another of the churches as the first to be formed or the first to have a building.[4] Overwhelming evidence indicates that all evolved about the same time at about the same rate. Evidently, all three had elected elders before or during 1784, and all were in worship regularly by 1785. When Rice refused to administer the Lord's Supper to any Kentucky Presbyterians because of what he perceived as their moral turpitude, he did not single out any particular church or mention their differing status.

Other congregations were formed in 1784: New Providence Church on the Salt River; Mt. Zion Church in Lexington; Paint Lick on Jessamine Creek; Pisgah Church about eight miles southwest of Lexington.[5] Congregations at Hopewell, at Salem, and at Whitley's Station/Crab Orchard also appeared in minutes of meetings as being in existence in July, 1785.[6] Each of the congregations naturally bore marks of individuality, and words about a few of the first serve to point out more leaders as well.

Concord Church at Danville soon became known simply as the Presbyterian Church of Danville. Many of its constituting families, including the John Caldwells, had come to Kentucky directly from Pennsylvania, although some of those had sojourned in Virginia. Others came from a variety of places. Typically, earliest records of the church, if kept, were lost at a later time. Bishop said that Danville possessed a

Presbyterian meetinghouse in 1784, but some gatherings took place in the "Court House." A newspaper advertisement of June 7, 1788, invited bids for constructing a building as a Presbyterian church, a "framed meeting house which is to be fifty feet long and forty feet wide. . . . "[7]

The congregation at Cane Run also constructed a place of worship in 1784, on land provided by John Haggin. Caleb Wallace and John Templin were both elders in that church.[8]

A great deal can be learned about the New Providence Church, begun in early 1785, because a member of the McAfee family wrote about its founding. He indicated that Rice had begun to preach on the banks of the Salt River, beginning in June, 1784.[9] The minister had also solemnized marriages and conducted a funeral there that year. In addition, he had "catechized" in the homes of "such as turned their attention to Religious Matters"—visited them and asked theological questions based, in part, on a mutual respect for the Westminster Standards. During the fall, new families came to join those already living in the area. The Buchanan and Armstrong families joined the McAfees and McCouns. Other individuals took an interest. Celebrating an early Spring in 1785, the gatherings became an organized church:

> The neighborhood concluded to erect a house for the Double purpose of a school house and meeting house accordingly the following heads of familys met on the Branch south of the Present N. Providence Church Viz.: James McAfee, James McCoun, Sr., William Armstrong, Robert McAfee, John McGee, George Buchannon, Saml. McAfee, James McCoun, Junr. For the purpose of selecting a place to build the house two places were named. James McAfee offered the present site and two acres of land and James McCoun offered the same near His Spring where Garet Browns house now stands 3/4 of a mile below—George Buchannon and George McAfee were the chief speakers and the matter was debated with considerable warmth and finally carried 7 to 5 in favor of the present situation and as soon as planting corn was over the neighborhood again met and built a log cabbin 20 feet by 28, on the side of the hill about fifty yards south of the west end of the Present Brick church in which the Revd. David Rice preached once a month for several years, and a school was also occasionally taught.[10]

The Fork of Dicks (Dix) River Church, which Rice also served for a while, became part of other congregations as settlers moved from one portion of the Bluegrass to another. Bishop indicates that Jacob Fishback took his slaves to this church, and presumably others did also.[11] Several of the churches give evidence of the attendance of slaves, while others display something of a negative attitude toward slavery.

It should not surprise historians that congregations and the courts of the church served as places of discipline for the lives of believers. Because Presbyterians considered God the Lord of all life, they considered it their responsibility to help fashion the family, the community, and the government in a Christian way. The intense personal piety of some first settlers, seeing the providence of God in provision of game to eat and subsequently writing private testimonies of praise, carried into public life as well. Cheaters or profaners of God must be excluded from partaking of the Lord's Supper and reformed in their ways as soon as possible. People who did not attend public worship with faithfulness were considered untrustworthy in matters commercial or legal.

The session, the representative gathering of lay leaders and their minister, the initial "court" in Presbyterian government, soon exercised judgment on all kinds of matters. For the most part, the session sought repentance and faithfulness among believers, although sometimes parochial interests took precedence.

One of the first elders in the Pisgah Church, William Scott, received discipline from the session of that church for allowing Methodist and Baptist preachers to use his home for the missionary activity. More commonly, ministers regularly examined members on moral matters, as well as on theological topics, before permitting them to partake of the Lord's Supper.[12]

Although congregations with their sessions bore distinctive marks, they shared much also in mutual goals and traditions. Presbyterians sought to base their worship on what they understood to be the worship patterns of the New Testament church. Their hopes remained tied to minimal changes from the styles of worship exhibited in the book of Acts.

By all accounts, exercises of public worship were usually very long. According to some, such worship provided richness and depth for Christian life; according to other sources, long services were merely tedious. Intimately linked with the desire to honor God on God's own day, and in light of Sabbath observance which allowed little else besides worship on Sunday, the services usually centered on "preaching," and frontier sermons lasted 90 minutes or more (if written versions of sermons corresponded to those actually delivered). Calvinism required the exposition of Scripture, the interpretation of the Word. Quite a bit was made of doctrine, with careful delineations of the meaning of "atonement," "regeneration," "perseverance of the saints," and "Christian duty," frequently themes for the sermons. Much also could be discussed with topics such as "heaven," "hell," and "conversion," honored subjects from the time of the Great Awakening. Every sermon, however, began with a text. Most of the time the exposition had something to do with the actual words of the passage.[13]

The longest services were celebrations called "sacramental occasions," following Scot traditions. Sometimes beginning with Saturday worship in preparation for the Sabbath, they usually consisted of an all-day affair of worship and preaching on Sunday. After an "action" sermon calling the faithful to communion, the members of the session would assist the minister, its moderator, in "fencing the table." Earlier the minister had issued communion tokens to those "worthy" of receiving the sacrament. These persons would present their tokens and be seated at tables for the words of institution, prayer of consecration, and distribution of sacrament. Since such occasions meant the gathering of the faithful, they could also serve as a time of infant baptism and adult confession of belief with baptism. The occasions frequently lasted all day Monday, as teaching and social times followed. Sacramental occasions came once or twice a year, strategically located in the farming cycle to provide maximum freedom from the tilling, weeding, and reaping.

If the sacramental occasions came seldom, regular worship came routinely. Presbyterians followed a middle way between the spontaneity of some Baptist church services and the strict ritual of the Catholics and Episcopalians. A *Directory of Worship,* authorized for the whole of the Presbyterian Church in 1788, may have provided more ritual than frontier congregations actually followed. But the items of worship probably corresponded in the order to those employed among early Kentucky Presbyterians: Prayer of Adoration, Invocation, Preparation, Reading of Scripture, Singing of Praise, Long Prayer of Adoration, Confession, Thanksgiving, Supplication and Intercession, the Lord's Prayer, Sermon, Prayer, Singing of a Psalm, Offering, and Blessing.[14]

Presbyterians inherited an anti-liturgical tradition from both English Puritanism and from the Scottish Church. Thus, for example, the only reading permitted was of the passage or passages pertinent to the sermon. In addition, the minister alone prayed aloud on behalf of the assembled faithful. Members of the congregation did not even repeat the Lord's Prayer out loud.[15]

Presbyterians lived out their piety in organization as well as in worship and work. Thus the sessions and pastors remained accountable at first to their respective Virginia courts.

Transylvania Presbytery

The nature of Presbyterian connectionalism meant that higher church courts must surely follow creation of new congregations in a distinct region. To attend the quarterly meetings of Abingdon Presbytery, to which Kentucky was assigned, would have proved impossible for ministers or elders desirous of doing more with their lives than riding horseback to and from Virginia. As soon as could be arranged, the leaders of new congregations met with ministers to form a presbytery. Organizational conferences took place on March 30 and July 12, 1785. At the first meeting, four preachers and ten lay representatives attended.[15] At the second, more elaborate meeting, two elders each attended from Walnut Hill, Mount Zion, Jessamine Creek, Mount Pisgah, Paint Lick, Fork of Dicks (Dix) River, Concord (Danville), Cane Run, New Providence, Hopewell, Salem, and the yoked congregations at Whitley's Station and Crab Orchard. David Rice and Adam Rankin were there, along with Terah Templin and James Crawford. Rice moderated both conferences, and Caleb Wallace twice served as clerk.[16]

The July conference requested formation of the new presbytery, and it likewise called for a day of "Fasting, Humiliation, and Prayer," on the first Wednesday of August, if possible. People were to focus upon "the dangers to which the country was still exposed from a savage enemy," and upon the task of ridding Kentucky of its "prevalence for vice." Elders in the congregations should lead the people in regular worship, even if ministers could not be present. The faithful should pray, read the Scripture, read some selections from standard works on theology, and sing hymns together.[17] In the second conference, and much more in the meetings of the presbytery which followed, the question about which hymns could be sung produced debate.

The first regular meeting of Transylvania Presbytery, held after the parent bodies gave consent to its formation, occurred on October 17 and 18, 1786. The first act of business was to seat formally Terah Templin as a member of the body. Presbytery heard "supplications" from forming congregations, requests for services by ordained clergy. They made plans for meeting the needs of various congregations, and they examined Thomas Meek, a candidate for ministry.[18]

Early meetings of the presbytery were filled with routine business of a frontier church, the assigning of pastors to preach and celebrate sacraments at the widely-separated churches, the examination of candidates, and the consideration of plans to form a General Assembly in the U.S. But the meetings also dealt with problems peculiar to the Kentucky situation—the decisions concerning church discipline on the frontier, the need for additional pastors, and the dispute between Adam Rankin and the rest of the body concerning church music.

The argument Rankin raised provided the presbytery with its first major test, and it showed just how tenuous and fragile frontier institutions were. It cut no new ground for the church, for it merely followed the previous hostilities which had taken place in New York City in the 1750s.

Rankin, together with many in his Lexington congregation, Mt. Zion Presbyterian, considered the literal translations of Psalms which had been authorized by Westminster divines in the 1640s to be the only renditions suitable for use in public worship.

Generally, seventeenth-century Scot Presbyterians had been accustomed to singing metrical versions of the biblical Psalms, literally translated by Francis Rous (1643). During the eighteenth century, most of the Presbyterians continued firmly in the same tradition. Under the influence of the English, however, whose *Bay Psalm Book* had been more eclectic, liberally paraphrased psalms with increasingly melodious tunes became fashionable among many American Presbyterians. Specifically, the metrical arrangements by Rous were giving way to the "Christian songs" of Isaac Watts and others.[19] Watts, the English nonconformist minister, had written some of the most appealing "new" hymns, such as "Bless, O My Soul, the Living God," based on Psalm 103; "O God Our Help in Ages Past," based on Psalm 90; and "Jesus Shall Reign Where'er the Sun," a Christo-centric statement following the general direction of Psalm 72. Even some Americans had written hymns that began finding their way into public worship during the "Great Awakenings" of the 1740s.[20]

The squabble erupted after smoldering for several years. Adam Rankin, in collaboration with some like-minded followers, revolted against the movement to sing a wider range of hymns in church. In the same meeting that considered Scott's appeal from session discipline at Cane Run on October 7, 1789, "sundry papers" presented a charge against Rankin that presbytery postponed hearing.[21] Rankin then went to the initial American General Assembly as a vociferous observer—not as a representative. The majority there affirmed the liberalization of tradition concerning hymns. They said, as had their Synodical predecessors, that congregations were free to choose metrical versions, but they were also free to choose other appropriate hymns.[22]

Returning to his Lexington congregations, Rankin began to bar from communion all those opposing his views on the subject. He cited as his authority for action both biblical admonitions on the matter, as well as his personal revelatory experiences, "dreams sent from God."[23] Presbytery appointed a committee to investigate the problem. Rankin took spring 1790 as an opportunity to leave Kentucky (and the whole U.S.) for a prolonged visit to London. The presbytery, meeting to consider the problem, postponed any trial of Rankin in his absence. After a full year, in April 1792, the presbytery finally did respond to the request of Pisgah people for an active and interested minister, suspended Rankin (after he withdrew) and declared the pulpit vacant that fall.[24]

By designed coincidence, Rankin left the presbytery to enter, in quick fashion, the Associate Reformed Church, an American wing of a Scottish communion agreeable to his exclusion of "Christian songs" from public worship.[25] Thus, the frontier presbytery was split, and other Presbyterian communions began to compete for the allegiance of the believers. Congregations of Presbyterians were variously affected by the departure of Rankin from the Transylvania Presbytery, and his embracing a communion not previously present in the area. Pisgah, Rankin's country congregation, evidently remained intact and relatively pleased to call James Blythe as their new pastor. He served that church for forty years, first as its pastor and then as stated supply.[26]

Meanwhile, Rankin's town church, Mt. Zion, joined him in the Associate Reformed Presbyterian denomination. Records indicate that the nearby congregation of New Providence divided over the matter, with James McCoun and John McGee elders in the "Rankinite" congregation that resulted. One McAfee remembered that the affair "continued to divide the people of Kentucky for several years," and produced "bickering and unpleasant feelings."[27] Not only did the presbytery lose one of its youthful and, by all accounts, most talented ministers with several hundred Reformed Christians, it likewise focused internally the energy and concern that could have been channeled elsewhere—into missions, for example.

Transylvania Presbytery attempted to discipline its members and the congregations that constituted it. In 1794, the ecclesiastical court ordered that young slaves held by Presbyterians should be taught "to read the Word of God" and prepared "for the enjoyment of freedom." All slaves should be instructed "in the principles and precepts of the Christian religion," and all masters should encourage slaves to attend worship. Two years later, the court called slavery evil but refused to bar slaves owners from communion.[28]

The discipline exercised by Transylvania Presbytery on its own members appears to have been exceedingly gentle. In April, 1798, charges were brought against the Reverend William Mahon by members of his congregation, the New Providence Church. A Mr. Samuel Dickey accused the preacher of "whipping unmercifully his Negro woman." When Dickey had relayed the information to George McAfee, an elder, McAfee had examined the woman and found "her skin cut in two places upon her left arm, and a hole in her right side." The trial of the complaint involved several other witnesses, for several pages of testimony are in the minutes, including a statement from one woman. Mary Wilson said Mahon's slave had bragged on having "her master in a good way now." If he beat her at all, she would make all the noise she could. In the end, the presbytery gave Mahon "a friendly admonition" to guard his temper.[29]

Presbyterians should have been experiencing youthful growth and a sense of vocation in those early years of their corporate life. The General Assembly, and the Synod of Virginia, encouraged the presbytery in such direction by sending missionaries, some of whom proved resilient and helpful to the cause of Reformed Christianity. At least one, William Calhoun, who came to Kentucky in 1792, soon returned to the comparative civilization offered by Virginia.[30] Most of the others remained, many having come with their full, extended families. John Poage Campbell, for example, one of the early students of Rice in Kentucky, served churches in Danville, Nicholasville, Cherry Spring, Versailles, and elsewhere.[31] Cary Allen was ordained pastor of the Paint Lick and Silver Creek Churches in 1794.[32] Robert Marshall, evidently one of the most capable of these missionaries, pastored the Bethel and Blue Springs churches before entering fully into the revival movement.[33] Robert Stuart had already served the Synod of Virginia as a missionary in the northern section of that state. He served a long pastorate in the Walnut Hill Church, east of Lexington.[34] One trustworthy historian, Davidson, counted eight missionaries in all, sent by the Synod to help spur the growth of Presbyterianism during the final years of the eighteenth century.[35] Their work, along with that of many lay and a few other ordained Presbyterians, resulted in the formation of approximately forty-five functioning congregations by the turn of the century.

The Synod of Kentucky

In March 1799, the Presbytery of Transylvania was divided into three distinct judicatories: Washington Presbytery, which covered the extreme eastern portion of the state together with areas to the north of the Ohio River; West Lexington Presbytery, in the middle between the Licking River and the Kentucky River; and the reduced Transylvania Presbytery, which still contained the areas to the south and west of the Kentucky River.[36]

These three courts made the requisite number to comprise a synod, and they were doubtless formed in order to make a Synod of Kentucky. As quickly as possible, they sought to form their own synod. The new Synod of Kentucky was designated as distinct from its parent, Synod of Virginia, in 1802. The first meeting of the new court took place at the Meetinghouse in Lexington on Thursday, October 14, 1802. David Rice, the semi-retired "Father" of the area's Reformed population, moderated the meeting, and he also preached the convocation sermon on Isaiah 8:20.

The new synod had its hands full from its very inception. The first of the Synod of Kentucky's substantial actions created a new Cumberland Presbytery, separating the western portion of Transylvania Presbytery, which lay to the south of the Salt River. By the time that presbytery met, the effects of the Great Revival sweeping the state were fully felt. At the second meeting of the Synod, in September 1803, ardent advocates and equally forceful skeptics of the revival fought fiercely over the direction the church should take. The Synod of Kentucky would experience the trauma of the frontier right away.[37]

In fact, the situation in the state had become quite chaotic. Resident population in Kentucky, for example, had almost tripled in ten years, between 1790 and 1800; it practically doubled again during the following decade. The first national census in 1790 had shown 74,000 Kentuckians, although on the frontier such statistics were of doubtful precision. The 1800 count declared that 221,000 lived in the state; the 1810 total, 407,000.[38] Many of the settlers came from ethnic backgrounds traditionally Presbyterian. But the Synod of Kentucky counted fewer than 2,000 members.[39]

One might describe the religious climate among Presbyterians as "confused and defensive," hardly the proper worldview in which to confront such a challenge. Some members and a few leaders had been lost in the Rankin controversy. Presbyterians did not know what to make of the revival which began among them. Students of revivalism still have trouble understanding and evaluating these fascinating events.

The congregations, sessions, presbyteries, schools, and the synod all remained frontier organizations. Their attempts to gain regularity in meetings and records remained thwarted by sheer logistics and by powerful forces of seeming chaos. Distances made gathering difficult and communication uncertain. Money, or rather the lack of it, forced ministers to rearrange their priorities in order to feed and clothe their families. Farming techniques sometimes starved the soil in marginal areas, forcing families to relocate on more fertile lands, usually to the west. The untimely deaths of parents put children in premature positions of responsibility, frequently destroying any chance of further formal education. The Presbyterian system, dependent upon literate laity and clergy who would give stable direction to mission activity, suffered.

Some congregations lacked the will to organize, and others elected sessions whose members died or migrated elsewhere. Some schools founded in one year disbanded the next when a teacher or a patron was lost to the venture. By 1802 some congregations had already dissolved. The Fork of Dicks River Church, for example, which at one time was among the strongest of the pioneer congregations, had ceased corporate worship by that year. Some of its members joined the Danville Church, some helped form another in Lancaster, and many moved to Missouri and Indiana.[40]

If Kentucky Presbyterians suffered, they also fed the frontier movement. Congregations in Cincinnati, Vincennes, and Nashville had their beginning when Kentuckians moved into Ohio, Indiana, and Tennessee. And while most of the members of the Synod of Kentucky lived in the Bluegrass area, by 1802 there were worshiping churches in Middletown, outside Louisville, and far to the west of the state in Livingston. Kentucky Presbyterians petitioned the General Assembly to send more missionaries to help organize more churches throughout the state.[41]

All Kentucky Presbyterians also shared in the struggle concerning control of Transylvania Seminary, which if it were not at the beginning an institution of Synod, nevertheless focused attention upon itself. In 1780, Presbyterians in Virginia, with the Reverend John Todd and his nephew Colonel John Todd among the leaders, had secured legislation to endow a ''Public School'' in Kentucky. Lands taken from ''British subjects'' were made available to trustees who might form a ''Seminary of Learning.''[42]

Transylvania Seminary had begun when David Rice, Caleb Wallace, Isaac Shelby, Christopher Greenup and Benjamin Logan, a quorum of the trustees, met near Danville in November 1783. The school actually held first classes in David Rice's log home, with James Mitchel as the sole teacher in 1785. When Mitchel moved back to Virginia, the school became a dormant institution for three years.[43]

In 1788, the trustees chose to relocate Transylvania in Lexington, home of Robert Patterson and Harry Innes, who by that time served on the board. They also hired Isaac Wilson to head the grammar school portion of the reincarnated school. James Moore replaced Wilson in 1791, and he continued as head of the lower school even though the Presbyterians failed to sustain his ordination examinations in 1792. As a consequence, Moore joined the Episcopal Church. He became the first permanent clergyman of that communion in the Bluegrass as the rector of Christ Church in Lexington.[44]

Presbyterian leaders who had failed to sustain Moore's examinations to become ordained felt the school slipping further from their control when in 1794 they saw Harry Toulmin elected president of the institution. Caleb Wallace had previously resigned, and Rice had retired, when critical questions had been voiced about Presbyterian control of a public institution. Now more resigned because they considered the election process illegal, Presbyterian leaders likewise considered Toulmin an "infidel."[45]

When Toulmin arrived in Lexington, he did represent "free thought" and he also embodied the aspirations of pro-French Kentuckians who considered the Presbyterians parochial. Embittered Presbyterians launched a rival Kentucky Academy at the Pisgah Church under Andrew Steele. David Rice and James Blythe, pastor of Clear Creek and Pisgah Churches, journeyed to the seaboard states to raise money while others moved to have the legislature in the new state appropriate land for the enterprise. Under Toulmin enrollment at Transylvania flagged, and he resigned in 1796.[46] The two schools merged quickly to become Transylvania University, still with a board independent of formal Presbyterian control but now more responsive to the church.[47]

Episcopalian James Moore was elected the first president of the newly-reorganized university in 1798. Appointments were made also in medical and law departments. James Blythe was chosen Professor of Mathematics and Natural Philosophy, while another Presbyterian minister, James Welsh, became professor of languages. Blythe responded well to the challenge and subsequently became Acting President when Moore resigned; but Welsh acted in an obnoxious fashion and student revolts against his censoriousness finally prompted his dismissal in 1801.[49]

Transylvania University, then, as a frontier institution, lived a very erratic life in its early years. The members of the Synod of Kentucky who had fought to regain control of it did not succeed in maintaining power for long.

The Rev. Gideon Blackburn (1772–1838), missionary to Cherokee Indians, who came to Kentucky and became President of Centre College. He also served churches in Louisville and Versailles before moving to Illinois.

Frequently congregations met in homes or meeting houses. Here is the Love House or Tavern in Frankfort, where that church was formed and where the state legislature also met in the 1790s.

CHAPTER 3.

The Great Revival

In the very first years of the nineteenth century a series of revivals took place in Kentucky. Spectacular by any measure, the revivals infused energy into the more settled eastern seaboard areas from the frontier. Men and women, particularly among the younger age brackets, "quit their meanness and joined the church" in record numbers. While the Methodists and Baptists gained dramatically in membership, and while the Christian Church (Disciples of Christ) and Cumberland Presbyterian Church were born in the revival, for the most part, Presbyterians themselves suffered division and disappointment![1]

Studies of the Great Revival are numerous and insightful. Recent scholars have declared a variety of causes for the phenomenon. Some have said the structure of encampment itself was conducive to emotional fervor, that an ethos for conversion was present, and that in responding to the preaching people found "release from tension." One particularly good study has focused on the "need to belong" that frontier people felt, and it argues that the Great Revival presented a society of heaven "where their troubles would end forever." At the same time, it identified belonging to the churches as a location in this life which corresponded to the eternal, otherworldly society.[2]

Whatever the general reasons for the success of the Great Revival, Kentucky Presbyterians began the movement, received its full impact, and were indelibly stamped in a negative fashion as a result of it.

Roots of Revival

Several special sources of the revival can be identified within Presbyterianism itself. The "Great Awakening" had provided an acceptable tradition for American Presbyterians by the turn of the nineteenth century. The eucharistic observance of a "sacramental occasion" gave a ready context for what transpired. Too, James McGready showed Kentucky Presbyterians that in fact a minister could be a Calvinist and a revivalist at the same time.

Most of the leadership of Kentucky Presbyterianism followed from the "New Side" heritage of colonial life which they claimed. In 1741, colonial American Presbyterianism had been divided over the "surprising work of God," the series of revivals which came to be called the "Great Awakening." The New Side embraced the emotional worship services, the itineration of clergy as evangelists, and the subsequent activism in piety issuing from conversion. It had included William Tennent, Sr., his sons Gilbert, John, and William, Jr., Samuel Blair, and a number of other ministers. While Old Side Presbyterians lamented the loss of theological precision in Calvinism and the decline of order in worship, New Siders offered the theology of Jonathan Edwards as a true and useful Reformed resource for the church.[3]

Samuel Davies, who had personally converted David Rice and who had exercised an almost patriarchal authority in colonial Virginia, had been a member of the New Side party during the split. When the split healed, in 1758, Davies and other New Side leaders had made the theology of Jonathan Edwards at least partially respectable. Even though subsequent migrations of Scotch-Irish had not been influenced by the New Side thought, and even though a conservative reaction took place in the Presbyterian Church during its formative period, nevertheless a large segment of the leadership in frontier Presbyterianism had permission to consider a revival potentially healthy in the new land.[4]

Both the spiritual children of New Side colonists and the tradition-minded Scotch-Irish shared a memory of the "sacramental occasion" as a positive experience. Together they sought to celebrate "sacramental occasions" on the frontier. The New Siders recalled how people had gathered for worship, and they remembered the celebration of the Lord's Supper with several preachers. The Scots, too, had known of long and disciplined procedures for "fencing the tables," concelebration with a number of clergy participating, and a period of communal fasting and prayer before the distribution of the sacrament to the faithful.[5]

Early reformers in the sixteenth century, such as John Calvin and John Knox, had sought to erase the popular, mechanical understandings of the sacraments. Though they had still advocated frequent observance of communion, other Protestants had prevailed and typically eucharist came to be a very unusual event. Ministers and sessions sought to prepare the people for the infrequent observance with seasons of fasting, prayer, repentance and rededication. They had examined the faithful following biblical admonitions to keep the unworthy from participating lest they destroy themselves in the process.[6]

One account of the Scot "sacramental occasion" at the close of the eighteenth century sounds almost identical to the plans for the first Kentucky camp meetings:

> The Sacrament is given once in the year (parishes still combined, though not on the previous scale—now usually only two or three parishes uniting): three discourses on the fast day, two on Sunday, two on Monday; the action sermon in the church, and the evening sermon, besides preaching in the tent. People have complained that the tent preaching was prejudicial. I am inclined to believe the contrary from experience: first, on account of its bringing a considerable collection for the poor; and secondly it accustoms a number of people to meet together in a decent, cheerful, and respectable manner.[7]

Reinforcing the tradition of the Great Awakening and the practice of the sacramental occasion came the person—James McGready. Born in western Pennsylvania, perhaps in 1760, McGready had been reared in the Scotch-Irish environment there, and subsequently in North Carolina when his family moved to Guilford County in 1778. He studied under several graduates of the College of New Jersey, and he himself experienced conversion at a sacramental meeting in Pennsylvania in 1786. Licensed to preach, McGready returned to his North Carolina home and began ministry there. Finding considerable resistance to the revivals he began at the Haw River and Stoney Creek churches, he moved in 1797 to Logan County, Kentucky to serve the Gasper, Muddy, and Red Rivers congregations forming in that vicinity.[8]

During the very spring (of 1797) in which McGready was received (without incident) in Transylvania Presbytery, the beginnings of a revival occurred in his congregations. A number of those who admired McGready, and who led the Presbyterians into the Great Revival, came into the state about the same time—William McGee, Barton Stone, and John Rankin among them.[9] People reacted with emotion to McGready's sermons, and the number of the faithful grew.

McGready, already known for his advocacy of repentance, faith, and regeneration, proved an acceptable colleague for other members of Transylvania Presbytery. He himself strongly affirmed the authority of the *Westminster Standards*, replete with their "hard doctrines" of predestination, total depravity, and irresistible grace. He viewed his revival preaching and the emotion-laden worship, especially for communion, as merely a continuation of the New Side dependence on the solid Calvinism of Edwards. From this perspective, McGready emphasized the power of hell, the promise of heaven, and the gift of faith for living a Christian life. However, as his apprentices saw, McGready did not shy away from those who emotionally experienced the impact of his words. On the contrary, McGready entered into covenants with them to require disciplined fasting and prayer "for the conversion of sinners."[10]

Spread of the Revival

Although McGready had already experienced some religious fervor in his congregations, and although dramatic conversions had occurred sporadically in Virginia, Pennsylvania, and North Carolina, the "Great Revival" began in 1800 among the Presbyterians at Gasper River, Red River, and Muddy River. In June, the Red River congregation held a sacramental occasion led by McGready, William Hodges, and John Rankin. John and William McGee also attended from Tennessee.[11]

Emotions intensified during the preparation services on Friday and Saturday, then a woman begged "What must I do to be saved?" in the middle of the Sunday service. Another screamed. The heat of religious fervor mellowed briefly on Monday, but then William McGee "went through the house shouting and exhorting with all possible ecstasy and energy, and the floor was soon covered by the slain."[12]

Encouraged by the conversions and the demonstrations of piety at Red River, anticipating even greater results at the Gasper River sacramental occasion, McGready and his colleagues advertised the July event and the first American camp meeting ensued. McGready remembered for the record that thirteen wagons remained on the grounds, having brought people and provisions. McGready invited Methodist ministers to share leadership with him, and several clergy led worship. "Ministers and private Christians were kept busy during the night," McGready reported, "conversing with the distressed." Later he was especially impressed with the cry of joy from a young girl:

> "Oh, he is willing, he is willing—he is come, he is come—O what a sweet Christ he is—O what a precious Christ he is—O what a fulness I see in him—O what a beauty. . . . "

The young girl then pled with the other sinners to repent "and all this in language so heavenly, and at the same time so rational and scriptural, that I was filled with astonishment."[13]

McGready administered the sacrament at tables which had been constructed from logs, and other logs provided material for an outdoor pulpit and pews to accommodate the crowds. He claimed that "forty-five souls were brought to Christ on this occasion."

The third congregation, Muddy River, held its sacramental occasion in August. The process repeated itself, with more planning. Friday night the people arrived. Preparation preaching and examination occurred on Saturday, the action sermon and communion on Sunday, catechesis or training sermons on Monday, and on Tuesday departure.

Presbyterians came from other congregations, too, and McGready convinced the skeptics among them of the efficacy of the experience. Other congregations invited him to conduct sacramental meetings at their churches—Shiloh, Hopewell-in-Cumberland, and even Red Bank across the Ohio.[14]

Revivals at sacramental occasions also took place in McGready's absence. Methodists at quarterly meetings, and Baptists, too, experienced similar effects. As word spread, so did the revivals—into Tennessee, North Carolina, Virginia, Pennsylvania, and the Northeast.[15]

Kentucky Presbyterians at first experienced the benefits of the harvest. The Reverend George Baxter of Virginia wrote that in 1801 in eastern Kentucky "the ministrations of the Presbyterian clergy began to be better attended than they had for many years before; their worshiping assemblies more solemn; and the people after they were dismissed showed a strange reluctance at leaving the place." Baxter, who spent several months visiting the area, concluded that the power of the revival had a great "influence in moralizing the people."[16]

Richard McNemar, who had been recently ordained by Transylvania Presbytery, reported on the sacramental meeting at Flemingsburg in April 1801, with its "weeping, trembling, and convulsion of soul." Again, "little girls" spoke to the sinners. At Cabin Creek, Mason County, he reported that "a new scene was opened." "While some trembled like one in a fit of ague, wept, or cried . . . others were employed in praying with them, encouraging them to believe. . . . " At Cabin Creek, McNemar declared "great numbers" fell. "To prevent their being trodden underfoot by the multitude, they were collected together and laid out in order, on two squares of the meetinghouse."[17]

The biggest and most effusive sacramental meetings took place that summer—in the Bourbon County Concord Church, Pleasant Point, and Cane Ridge. McNemar described the Concord camp meeting in some detail:

> The number of people was supposed to be about 4,000, who attended on this occasion. There were present seven Presbyterian ministers; four of whom were opposed to the work, and spoke against it until the fourth day about noon; the evidence then became so powerful, that they all professed to be convinced, that it was the work of God; and one of them addressed the assembly with tears, acknowledging, that notwithstanding they had long been praying to the Lord, to pour out his spirit, yet when it came, they did not know it; but wickedly opposed the answer of their own prayers. On this occasion, no sex or color, class or description, were exempted from the pervading influence of the Spirit; even from the age of eight months, to sixty years, there were evident subjects of this marvelous operation.
>
> The meeting continued five days, and four nights; and after the people generally scattered from the ground, numbers convened in different places, and continued the exercise much longer. And even where they were not collected together, these wonderful operations continued among every class of people, and in every situation; in their houses and fields, and in their daily employments, falling down and crying out, under conviction, or singing and shouting with unspeak-

able joy, were so common, that the whole country round about seemed to be leavened with the spirit of the work.[18]

Without doubt the most famous of the camp meetings took place at Cane Ridge, in Bourbon County, for the sacramental occasion of August 1801. Its organizer, the Reverend Barton Stone, had joined Transylvania Presbytery in October 1798. Stone had attended Guilford Academy in North Carolina, when he had been converted after hearing McGready and William Hodge. Stone had made his way to Kentucky, after licensure in North Carolina, to become the pastor of the Concord and Cane Ridge Churches. In July 1801, only a month before the meeting, he had married Elizabeth Campbell.[19]

Stone put the number of participants at between 20,000 and 30,000. Others estimated anywhere from 12,000 to 50,000 were in attendance. Eighteen presbyterian ministers were there, in addition to perhaps an equal number of Baptist and Methodist clergy. By every account, the events proved dramatic, and the meeting stretched to consume six full days.[20]

Stone remembered, "Four or five preachers were frequently speaking at the same time, in different parts of the encampment without confusion. . . . Many things transpired there, which were so much like miracles, that if they were not, they had the same effects as miracles on infidels and unbelievers. . . . "[21] John Lyle, who preached also at Cane Ridge, did perceive confusion; he discussed the problem with the Reverend James Blythe. But Lyle was interrupted in his analysis by word that another unnamed colleague "had fallen." He, Blythe, James Welsh, Robert Marshall and Rankin all experienced deep personal emotion, "Blythe immoderately."[22]

Many participants experienced a variety of physical "exercises," described in a catalog of "bodily agitations" Stone named the "falling," the "jerks," the "dancing exercise," "barks," "laughing" and "singing" exercises.[23] Peter Cartwright, the Methodist, also described the jumping exercise, but he enjoyed particularly the "jerks." It excited his "risibilities," he confessed, "to see those proud young gentlemen and young ladies, dressed in their silks, jewelry and prunella, from top to toe, take the jerks."[24]

The high point of the occasion, at least as far as Presbyterians were concerned, was that the sacramental tables on Sunday were set for several hundred communicants. In a personal diary, Lyle recalled his own involvement in the examination and the distribution of the elements:

> I went in among a cluster of rejoicers and shook hands with some of them, one stood staring like he saw Christ in the air, I asked him what views he had of Christ. He said he saw a fullness in him for all that come. Their looks were joyful but their appearance rather light but I cannot describe it. I went from them to the Communion, and sat down at the first table which Mr. Blythe served. I had some reviving clearer, views of divine things than I had before. In time the tables were serving Mr. Samuel Finley preached on how shall we escape, if we neglect so great salvation. I heard a part of that and then went to serve tables. When I spoke I felt uncommonly tender & c. There were eleven hundred communicants, according to the calculation of one of the elders others say better than eight hundred. [sic][25]

From the other side of the table, from one who received the elements at Cane Ridge, the episode changed his whole life.

Thomas Cleland of Washington County, Kentucky, had arrived in Lexington in October, 1799, just as a ''Sacramental Occasion'' was to take place. In preparation he had been reading the classic treatise . . . *On Religious Affections* by Jonathan Edwards and he had been praying. ''I thought perhaps were I to take the sacrament, it would produce that tenderness of feelings the absence of which I had so long lamented.'' Cleland did not receive any rigorous examination from the minister, however, and got a token just for the asking. When he turned it in and partook in the service, he expressed a keen sense of disappointment. He had remained relatively unaffected by the whole experience.[26]

> As to myself, I had fancied, that no sooner than I would reach the place and enter the religious atmosphere, I would enjoy quite a different feeling from that which I had so long experienced and lamented. I expected to fall quite soon, or experience some softening, pleasing, inward ecstasy—something I could not tell what. But, to my great disappointment, I felt unmoved, cold, and hard as stone.[27]

When Clelend subsequently attended the great gathering at Cane Ridge, though, he finally experienced a full measure of emotional results. After worrying all night, he arose to hear the ''action sermon'' on Sunday given by Robert Marshall, a favorite of the young man's among all the Presbyterian preachers. Cleland at last found what he had been looking for—"My heart was melted! My bosom heaved! My eyes, for the first time were fountains of tears." Cleland braced himself against a bench to keep from falling, and he said he felt "an indescribable sensation, as when one strikes his elbow against a hard substance." Ironically, Cleland became so emotional that he could not make it to the actual communion service going on nearby. But he considered his experience a kind of sacrament—"something like it had, all along, been so much desired, that I seemed to covet its uninterrupted continuance."[28]

There were in Cleland's case extenuating circumstances which may have served to increase his sense of involvement and his expectations concerning the meeting. His father had just died, and added to the process of grief were undoubtedly feelings of guilt for having been absent at the death bed. Then, too, Cleland fully expected to become a minister himself, and probably looked to the preachers as apprentices view masters in the trade they seek to learn. But thousands of other persons were radically affected, and many of them evidenced more dramatic results, both in the extent of their exotic reactions and in their changed lives afterwards.

After Cane Ridge, news of the revivals spread even more widely. Other occurrences multiplied, and James Fishback, on his way to Lexington in the fall of 1802, said he heard "of little else" than the Great Revival. Some ministers and lay people saw in the revival the first fruits of a coming millenium. Others began to institute the camp meetings at regular intervals. Scholars see in the movement of the revival thoughout the South a beginning of the powerful "Bible belt" in the region. Reactions to such a phenomenon occupied the frontier Presbyterians and caused fierce divisions among them.

Presbyterian Reactions

The Great Revival epitomized frontier religion in general, and frontier Kentucky Presbyterianism in particular. Raucous and confusing, yet full of spiritual vitality, the revival forced people to come to terms with it. At the center of social life, it "exercised" everyone. Some were "exercised" in religious experience, falling or dancing, barking or rolling. Many more "melted," a euphemism for crying and sobbing. Some folk "exercised," though, in more impious fashion, hustling and conniving participants into parting with money in exchange for corn whiskey, patent medicine, or a number of surrogates for either.

Others exercised their freedom from the normal patterns of social isolation and familial restraints. They maintained arguments or harangues among themselves or with whoever happened to be preaching, or they slipped away with a suitor into the surrounding woods. Some did not bother to slip away, and one meeting was interrupted when a couple (or more) was discovered in immodest condition under the boards of the elevated pulpit area.[29]

With all this and much more happening, it is no wonder that many people congregated at the camp meetings, and for a whole range of reasons. Meetings offered quite a contrast to the normal routine. Primarily, though, camp meetings and the revival movements were occasions for religious experience—conversion if need be, or, more likely, just for spiritual refreshment.

Some Presbyterians continued to count primarily the benefits of the revival. They discounted the hucksterism and the loose morality of the peripheral hangers-on, posted a watch to police the fringes, and proceeded to institutionalize the phenomenon as the Methodists and some Baptists did. Other Presbyterians lamented increasingly the loss of discipline for worshipful sacramental observance, despised the "thin gruel" that passed for theology, and considered an already embattled Calvinism worth defending whatever the cost. Still others, perhaps most, Presbyterians in Kentucky wanted to adapt both Calvinism and the unruly mass worship experiences to make a winsome Christianity for the new land.

The most thorough proponents of the revival movement called themselves "New Lights." In the words of McNemar, one of the leaders, "All creeds, confessions, forms of worship, and rules of government, invented by men, ought to be laid aside, especially the distinguishing doctrines of Calvin." All who received the "true light of the spirit in the inner man" and followed it would agree in obvious, spiritual truth.[30] McNemar believed that he did not repudiate Presbyterianism. Instead, the new, inclusive revival illumination merely revealed that tradition had been only partially true to the faith.

That McNemar still considered himself Presbyterian in 1803 is obvious in his reaction to the examinations instituted by his presbytery—

the newly-created Washington Presbytery, the area northeast of the Licking River and extending into Ohio. When he and a colleague John Thompson were accused of teaching the Arminian heresy, and a petition to the second meeting of the Synod of Kentucky, September 1803, charged that Washington Presbytery had not completed a process for judging the matter, McNemar, Thompson and John Dunlavy, Robert Marshall, and Barton Stone withdrew from Synod jurisdiction to form another, Springfield Presbytery.[31]

By official account, the Synod tried to reconcile differences with the departing portion of its membership.[32] According to McNemar, however, the Synod sought to excommunicate the dissidents instead of allowing them to leave the body peacefully.[33]

The formation of an independent Presbytery of Springfield by the five ministers and several congregations sympathetic to their revival theology offered a real threat to the whole of Presbyterianism in its structure and its connectional form. *Minutes* from the Turtle Creek Church, at the time the strongest in the Ohio region, illustrate the nature of the threat. "We think it the privilege of the Church mutually to profess their regard to the Holy Scriptures, as the only rule of faith and practice, the only standard of doctrine and discipline."[34] In moving into Springfield Presbytery, the Turtle Creek Church and its session affirmed the Reformed doctrine of the authority of Scripture. But they contrasted its authority with that of the Reformed standards, where traditionally Presbyterians had seen no (or little) discrepancy. Thus they moved against a major tenet in Reformed Christianity in the name of another major tenet, and they employed some of the very words f the *Confession of Faith* in order to repudiate it.

According to both proponents and opponents of the "New Lights," the powerful personalities of the new group and the winsomeness of their ways in putting forth their case split many of the congregations affected by the revival. Strong congregations at Paint Lick and Silver Creek, for example, served by Matthew Houston at this time, joined the new movement with their pastor.[35]

Significant numbers of Presbyterians agreed with Stone. "So low had religion sunk, and such carelessness universally had prevailed, that I have arrested the attention of the world; therefore these uncommon agitations were sent for a purpose."[36]

The coalition forming the new presbytery, recognizing only biblical authority, simply could not hold for long. Why develop another Presbyterian structure in order to repudiate the structure of Presbyterianism? In June 1804, the body composed and implemented a "Last Will and Testament of the Springfield Presbytery." They resolved the anomaly in a stroke of ironic wit. They willed that "this body die, be dissolved, and sink into union with the body of Christ at large. . . . " They poked some final barbs at their parent Synod:

> *Item. We will*, that the people henceforth take the Bible as the only sure guide to heaven; and as many as are offended with other books, which stand in competition with it, may cast them into the fire. . . . *Item. We will* that the Synod of Kentucky examine every member, who may be suspected of having departed from the Confession of Faith, and suspend every such suspected heretic immediately; in order that the oppressed may go free, and taste the sweets of Gospel liberty. . . .[37]

Hencefore a movement would replace a series of church courts. The believers became known simply as "Christians" rather than as Presbyterians. Cooperation soon broke down, though, as some Christians moved toward radical lifestyles and Christian communism. Shaker missionaries helped them along. Elders Seth Youngs, Issachar Bates, and John Meacham visited the western areas for the Shakers, appealing to Scripture and the expectant lifestyle it advocated as bases for embracing "The Society of Believers in Christ's Second Appearing." Houston and Stone first received the Shaker missionaries, and then recommended them to McNemar and the Turtle Creek Church across the river in Ohio, where experimentation with Christian communitarianism was already underway. Malcolm Worley and his family were the first to convert to Shakerism in the West. Worley, an elder and stalwart of the Turtle Creek Church, held several parcels of land nearby. Anna Middleton, a black woman in the congregation, evidently followed the Worleys into the newly forming community. McNemar and his wife Jane also became Shakers. Youngs wrote in his journal of the first "society meeting," May 23, 1805:

> After speaking, we sung an hymn, and while singing the following.
> With him in praises we'll advance
> And join the virgins in the dance.

> Jane McNemar got exercised in dancing for some time. . . . Richard also got to dancing and P. (Polly) Kimball, a woman of 27. . . .[38]

Conversions increased, and Turtle Creek became the center of the western mission of Shakerism. McNemar accompanied Youngs to Harrodsburg and Danville, where a Shaker mission in the heart of Kentucky took hold nearby. In time, John Dunlavy joined, as did Matthew Houston and numbers of other former Presbyterians. Most, including the three ministers, had moved through the "Christian" movement into a Utopian community based on the Acts of the Apostles and the theology of Mother Ann Lee.[39]

The same Christian movement that provided the Shakers with the bulk of their early western adherents also gave the missionaries of Mother Ann's colonies the most vocal opposition. Barton Stone and John Thompson in particular inveighed against the Shaker doctrine of celibacy and their belief that the millenium had begun. Thompson eventually reunited the Presbyterians; and Stone led one strong segment of the Christian Church into union with O'Kellyite Methodists, Campbellites and others to form a viable denomination. Eventually, the Disciples of Christ (Christian) Church resulted. Stone and members of the Presbyterian clergy, especially Thomas Cleland, printed hostile correspondence for several years; therefore Stone not only debated with adversaries on his left, but those on his "right" as well.[40]

Estimating the strength of the "Christian" movement remains an extremely difficult task. One list of congregations has been offered as the roll of "Springfield Presbytery" and the nucleus of Stone's followers in Kentucky: "Cane Ridge, Bourbon County; Republican, Bethel, and Mt. Tabor, Fayette County; Indian Creek, Harrison County; and Cabin Creek, Lewis County."[41]

The strength, then, of those Presbyterians who embraced the revivals and their fruits in Kentucky proved considerable. Many other Presbyterians came increasingly to criticize the revivals and to throw most of the power of the judicatories against them. A few of the clergy had reacted early in negative fashion to the upheavals. Rice, formally retired from his pastoral duties by 1801, had gone in September of that year to one sacramental occasion at Walnut Hill. The old minister arose in the pulpit, and exhorted the enthusiasts: "Holy, Holy, Holy! is the Lord God Almighty!" Rice had advocated separate sleeping arrangements for men and women, a night watch, and shorter periods of meeting. His views evidently did not carry among the leadership.[42]

John Lyle, too, began to criticize openly the camp meetings and their "extravagances."[43] Historians have generally considered these ministers, together with the majority of members in the Synod of Kentucky to be "anti-revivalists."[44] Actually, Rice and Lyle both had a rather positive view of revivals. Rice had experienced personal conversion, and Lyle had been "melted" at Cane Ridge. They, and others who joined them, opposed the sacrifice of doctrine at the altar of conversion experience. They considered worship a solemn affair, and they worried when the unexamined received the sacraments.

While they reacted with some vehemence to the threat of the Springfield Presbytery schism and its issue in a Shaker presence and a Stoneite movement, many Kentucky Presbyterians reacted negatively also to those among them who sought to gain a combination of Calvinism and revival enthusiasm. Most of these Presbyterians belonged to the new Cumberland Presbytery formed by the Synod in the southern portion of the state.

The attempts of a majority of the members of Cumberland Presbytery were to soften the harshest statements of Calvinism, to continue the revivals wherever possible, and to assign pastoral leadership quickly to the new congregations as they formed. The movement by Cumberland Presbytery to license "catechists," church assistants to serve in remote areas, had been suggested by Rice himself. But when the number of catechists increased dramatically and ordination of several licentiates occurred without their having received a liberal arts education, a minority of members of the presbytery complained to the Synod of Kentucky.[45]

In its very first meeting, for example, Cumberland Presbytery licensed Robert Guthrie, Robert Houston, Matthew Hall, and Samuel Hodge as exhorters and catechists. In addition, the new presbytery reaffirmed the decision of its parent Transylvania Presbytery to license John Hodge, Finis Ewing, Samuel King, and Alexander Anderson as preachers. Subsequent meetings of Cumberland Presbytery in 1804 brought decisions to ordain Ewing, King and Hodge along with other probationers. At the same time a number of additional exhorters were licensed. Thomas Craighead objected to the Synod of Kentucky, October 1804, that educational and theological requirements had not been met by the presbytery in its process of licensure and ordination.[46]

Synod responded by assigning a committee to attend a meeting of the presbytery. Archibald Cameron did go to a meeting of the presbytery. Meanwhile Cumberland Presbytery continued to license and to ordain ministers freely, so that by fall, 1805, there were twenty full members of the court and almost as many licentiates.[47] Synod that fall voted to reexamine the new members of Cumberland Presbytery, arguing that irregularities in the minutes of the body cast suspicion on the proceedings.

The commission first tested James Hawe, although his membership had been in Transylvania Presbytery before the Cumberland Presbytery formed. The commission proceeded to test the qualifications of twenty-two exhorters, ordinands and licentiates. Most, including King, McAdow, Ewing, Hodge, and Nelson, were prohibited from preaching until they submitted to the jurisdiction of Synod and received examination in all requisite areas of study and experience.[48]

After the commission acted, members of Cumberland Presbytery objected to the General Assembly that only a presbytery has the right to examine and license. Meanwhile the Synod of Kentucky dissolved the presbytery, reassigning ministers of longer tenure and effectually invalidating recent ordinations and licensures.[49]

The General Assembly of 1808 responded to the ex-members of the Cumberland Presbytery, declared that they were apparently entitled to relief, but that only the Synod could declare a presbytery constituted for recognition on the floor of the Assembly, and no sentiment (or vote) could help the Cumberland Presbyterians.[50]

A few of the leaders—James McGready and William Hodge among them—did capitulate to the decision of Synod. Most of the Cumberland pastors, however, and many lay leaders formed an independent Cumberland Presbytery.

Robert Davidson, defensive in his appraisal of the Presbyterian reaction to the revival, claimed that very few of the pastors and churches took part in it, that "New Lights" were nothing but schismatics, and that the persons ordained and licensed by Cumberland Presbytery were "illiterate exhorters with Arminian sentiments." Wrong on every score, Davidson proved most damaging in his appraisal of the Cumberland leaders. His characterization has remained the prevalent one in assessments of the movement.[51]

Most of the Cumberland leaders, Ewing and McAdow for example, possessed approximately the same liberal arts education as those who excised them from the church. At stake was a difference of opinion over the sequence of licensure, ordination, and education. More significant, at stake was Cumberland leaders' approbation of the revival's enthusiasm, versus the desire on the part of others to keep control of the Synod in the hands of people with a more "balanced" view of its nature and effects.[52]

As for the "Arminianism," Cumberland leaders did not soften language about election, atonement, effectual calling, and the perseverance of the saints when they adopted a Confession of Faith in 1814. But the argument against the stronger language of some chapters of the *Westminster Standards* could have been voiced within Presbyterianism without rupture of the body—indeed the debate did take place in other locations.[53]

So the Cumberland Presbyterian Church was cut off from the Synod of Kentucky, but it flourished on its own. And frontier Presbyterianism quickly became border institutions. Much of the fervor disappeared, but at least within the congregations of the Synod of Kentucky contentiousness remained. Presbyterians contended with others, while they also fought among themselves. In "border Presbyterianism," the story continues.

PART II.
Border

The Rev. James McChord (1785–1820), an early minister who moved from the Associate Reformed Presbyterian into the Presbyterian Church, U.S.A.

The Rev. John C. Young (1803–1857), pastor of Second Presbyterian Church, Lexington, and of Centre College in Danville. An educator and administrator, he helped with the founding of the Danville Theological Seminary in 1853.

CHAPTER 4.

Border Conflicts

During the period between the end of the "frontier" and the coming of the Civil War, Presbyterians did increase in members, organize churches in most urban areas of the state, give some support to missions elsewhere, and maintain a place of importance in the economic and social life of Kentucky. But they fought fiercely over matters connected with the institution of slavery, over the place of voluntary societies in church life, and they managed to divide again—into Old and New School synods. Other Presbyterian bodies, Cumberland and Associate Reformed, were not so much in the middle of Kentucky's issues and leadership, although the number of Cumberland Presbyterians increased significantly.

As in other "border" states, the matters connected with slavery preoccupied Kentuckians during the antebellum period. The numbers of slaves grew in each census period between 1790 and 1860, and they constituted about 20% of the state's population in each decade between 1810 and 1860.[1] Free black people also increased in number, though only in 1850 did they constitute even one percent of the state's population.[2] Kentucky's heritage in Virginia pulled the area toward the worldview of a slave economy. But the proximity of Kentucky to the free states of Indiana and Ohio, together with other factors, mitigated the effects of the institution in the state and helped maintain anti-slavery sentiments within Kentucky perspectives.[3]

Congregations and Institutions

The Presbyterian Church in Kentucky continued to grow, though at a far slower pace than did the Methodist and Baptist Churches. New Presbyterian congregations formed—in Frankfort, Maysville, Ashland, Louisville, and other communities where towns and cities arose. Predominantly rural congregations continued to hold sway, though, in determining much of the business of the ecclesiastical courts. Churches in the cities fought just to survive much of the time. But issues of substance did occupy the church and cause considerable friction, sometimes division, within congregations. And leaders of ante-bellum Presbyterianism repeatedly engaged in controversy.

In the Frankfort area, Presbyterians had formed the Upper Benson, or Hogsett, Church in 1795 in the home of Thomas Paxton. Another congregation had arisen about 1805 as the Lower Benson Church. But a Presbyterian church in the capital proper did not begin until 1816, when Thomas Paxton himself moved his membership into the new congregation. Other elders came also from country churches and the first membership roll, 1825, showed fifty-nine members, forty-five of whom were women.[4]

In the Ashland area, the Bethesda Presbyterian Church was organized in June 1819, in the log home of Major James Poage. Twenty members were received into the church that day, most of them Poages. A brick church building was constructed on land given by Elder George Poage, and the first regular pastor, the Reverend Charles Phillips, arrived in 1830. According to a local historian, Mrs. D. F. Myers, by the time the city of Ashland was laid out in 1854, the church "had received into its membership two hundred and thirty persons, and the names are almost a directory of anyone of consequence in the area."[5] A Presbyterian church in Maysville was formed from the Washington Church nearby, in June 1817. The Reverend Robert Wilson of the Washington Church served as temporary pastor of the new congregation until a regular pastor could be secured. The Reverend John T. Edgar was elected to that responsibility in 1820, and he served for about seven years. The first building, "an imposing structure painted a deep blue," burned in 1850; the congregation worshiped in the Methodist church (South) until the replacement was finished in 1852.[6]

A Presbyterian church in Middletown and another south of it at Pennsylvania Run had been established in frontier times. But it was not until January 1816, that Reformed Christians in Jefferson County organized themselves into a ''Presbyterian Society'' in Louisville, by that time a bustling city. Cuthbert Bullitt, Archibald Allen, John Gwathmey, Paul Skidmore, Joshua Heddington, and Alexander Pope were listed as leaders of the society as it moved to become a particular church a year later. The Reverend Daniel Banks, who had held worship for the society, helped raise funds for the new church building, and he became the minister at $900 per annum (for half his time). H. McMurtrie, in his 1819 *Sketches of Louisville*, described the edifice as ''neat, plain and spacious.'' It was ''furnished with galleries and an organ loft, the interior being divided into pews, intersected by three aisles. . . .''[7]

Banks encountered difficulty from fellow members of the Presbytery of Louisville, and he retired from the active pastorate in 1820. Several pastors served briefly in First Church, but none lasted long in the job. The congregation struggled for a whole decade before it achieved stability. And in 1830, a Second Presbyterian Church was founded in the city.[8]

The organization of town churches was accompanied by the initiation of some programs in congregations. The first ''Sabbath,'' or ''Sunday'' schools in the state, for example, formed as a result of the concern of Frankfort Presbyterians. At Frankfort, where tradition held that the second Sunday school in America was founded, the religious education of young people preceded the formation of a congregation.[9]

In 1810, the Reverend Michael Arthur from Scotland opened a school for boys in Frankfort, supported by the family of John Brown and others who belonged to the two Benson congregations. Mrs. Margaretta Brown urged Arthur to gather his students and any other boys who would come for Sunday lessons on catechism and Bible. The congregational history records that though Arthur left before Smith came as the first pastor of the First Presbyterian Church, the Sunday school proceeded for boys and another opened for girls in 1819. The history names Mrs. Brown as ''superintendent, secretary, and treasurer'' of the Sunday school; Mrs. Elizabeth Love, Mrs. Berkley, Miss Elizabeth Humphries, Mrs. Foster, and Mrs. Bush as early teachers. The schools met in the Love House, also called the Love Tavern, where the first sessions of the Kentucky legislature had been held.[10]

In 1826, the Sunday schools moved into the new church building which had been recently completed. Mrs. Brown and the other leaders took that occasion to reorganize the schools, as Methodist and Baptist churches began holding their own classes. The girls and boys joined in simultaneous classes, though they remained in separate groups. The Sunday school, as it became more closely tied to First Presbyterian Church, initiated a "society" to aid in educating poor children in the town.[11]

As other Sunday schools grew, they too frequently initially existed independently from session and ministerial control. Stalwart leaders in local congregations likewise began Sabbath schools for children. In similar fashion, women began to meet during the 1820s and 1830s in sewing, missionary, and Bible study groups. They learned about needs of missionaries, sewed clothes for the poor, and read the Bible together. Significantly, some congregations and some pastors resisted even these loose organizations during "border" times, fearing perhaps that the independent bodies would siphon interest and loyalty from the church.[12]

Preachers were wont to preach on correct and orthodox doctrines, to warn the faithful against error and disobedience. Respected ministers varied in their use of the Bible, sometimes following verses closely and at others "proving doctrine" by occasional reference to the Bible. Published sermons from two Kentucky ministers illustrate the range of their rhetoric.

James McChord, who opened the Market Street Presbyterian Church in Lexington in 1815, quoted at least two score verses and alluded to even more scriptural characters when he preached on the sovereignty of God. But his crucial, topical sentences argue that "God is omnipresent," "God is the great reality—the only stable and underived existence," and "This is the use his Bible teaches you to make of the doctrine of his omnipresence." Words of logic, "if . . . then," "adduce," "assumptions," and "inference" make the argument. Similarly, other sermons in McChord's repertoire sought to prove the true and to expose the false in doctrine.[13]

Lewis Green, who preached at Shelbyville and later at Danville, spoke "with freedom and fire" according to his biographer and he sometimes used frequent passages of Scripture to prove his point. "The

Resurrection of Christ,'' or ''Paul's Zeal for Israel and Its Lessons'' give thorough attention to Scripture. More frequently, however, he would seek to establish the doctrine of the text,'' as he sought to do for Psalm 53:1 in his sermon, ''The Sin and Folly of Atheism.'' Typically he would give transitions in the sermon in logic and proposition:

> And now, having endeavored to illustrate and confirm, by various examples, the doctrine of our text, we would direct your attention to one important deduction that may be drawn from the whole, namely, the importance and reasonableness of the doctrine of justification by faith.[14]

He would marshall evidence, refute objections, and conclude with deductions. Other such sermons included ''The Grounds on Which Men Reject the Gospel,'' ''Does God Always Punish Sin?'' and ''The Necessity of Regeneration.''

Preachers and laity likewise remained hostile towards institutions which seemed to indulge in error or promulgate it. Thus, for example, when Transylvania University did not prosper under the ministrations of James Blythe, the Board of Trustees moved in 1816 to make Horace Holley president of the school. Presbyterians learned that Holley professed Unitarianism, and heard it for themselves when he preached at the Market Street Church. The state legislature added insult to injury when it removed several Presbyterian dissidents from the Board and replaced them with people such as Henry Clay and Robert Wycliffe.

Presbyterians retaliated by establishing yet another institution for higher education—Centre College in Danville in 1819. More than anyone else, Samuel K. Nelson led the effort to charter Centre as a state institution which still provided that ''no religious doctrines peculiar to any one sect of Christians shall be inculcated by any professor in said college.'' In this effort, Presbyterians again found scant satisfaction; they soon moved to hold the reigns of Centre College much more tightly in the hands of the Synod of Kentucky.

In cities and towns, churches and institutions continued to come into being, and the importance of pastoral leadership may have been even more significant than in previous decades. There were, of course, those who served the churches without causing controversy. The Reverend Mr. Edgar, for example, had a good reputation as an orator when he pastored the Maysville church. Then he moved quietly to serve the

Frankfort church, and he rescued it from being in a "confused and disorganized condition, 1827–1833."[15] But he did not engage in much of the denominational warfare that characterized the period.

Isaac Bard, too, son of William and Mary Bard, received ordination in Muhlenburg Presbytery in 1823 and served as pastor of the Greenville, Mt. Zion, and Mt. Pleasant Churches for more than a decade. He then became a missionary and the financial agent for the presbytery, 1835–78. He could not avoid some of the conflicts which occurred during his ministry. But records intimate that he sought to make peace when possible and to reduce friction among warring parties when disputes arose.[16]

Pastors who received the fame, or the notoriety, in Kentucky during the antebellum period were those who proved to be especially contentious. Thomas Cleland, the "dean" of the disputants, moved into ministry out of the "Great Revival," and then led Presbyterian debunking of the "Christian" movement of Stone and Alexander Campbell. Cleland became the pastor of the New Providence and Cane Run Churches in 1813, he oversaw the move of the latter to become the Harrodsburg Presbyterian Church, and he wrote several tracts, such as "The Socini-Arian Detected, a Series of Letters to Barton W. Stone," (1815), and "Strictures on Campbellism," (1833).[17] Cleland also became the focus of a New School Synod in Kentucky, when it was separated from the Old School in 1836–38.

Cleland participated, indeed he led, in two major "border" battles of Kentucky Presbyterianism. But it should be noted that he commanded respect from almost all who knew him well, and he claimed that he remained a reluctant and shy disputant. He said he never spoke on the floor of a General Assembly to which he was delegate, and he attended many as such.[18]

Another pastor, Nathan L. Rice, loved to fight. He too grew up in Kentucky and he made his mark in the state before moving to Cincinnati in 1845, to lead the Central Presbyterian Church. Rice, born of a farming family in Garrard County in 1807, attended and taught at Centre College.[19] In 1833 he was ordained to lead the Bardstown Presbyterian Church. There Rice almost immediateiy established himself as a controversialist as well. He joined in a public accusation of irregularities and improprieties at a convent in the town. A priest, the Reverend George

Elder, President of St. Joseph's College at Bardstown, sued Rice in Nelson County Court. The jury awarded damages of one penny to the Catholics. Both litigants published one-sided histories of the lawsuit, and Rice included in his version some gratuitous comments against "Celibacy" and "Nunneries."[20]

In 1841, Rice moved to become a roving missionary for Ebenezer Presbytery. He worked primarily in the Paris Church, Bourbon County, and in the Woodford County Church after the Versailles and the Harmony Churches had separated from it. Rice became the official spokesperson for the presbytery in a "Great Debate" (so-advertised) with Alexander Campbell, leader of the Christians. With great fanfare the debate took place in Lexington, Kentucky, in November 1843. Henry Clay, aspiring to be President of the U.S. as the Whig Candidate of 1844, presided over portions of the event. Campbell and Rice did not settle the matters under discussion—infant and believer baptism, and the nature of creeds—but hundreds of Christians and Presbyterians could see their champions in combat, hear their own theologies affirmed in good grammar, and receive a full sixteen days of entertainment at the same time.[21] Rice later served as Moderator of the Old School Assembly, and he became pastor of the Fifth Avenue Presbyterian Church in New York City during the Civil War.

Without doubt the most important pastor during the period was Robert J. Breckinridge. He also proved the most irascible, the most frequent party leader in whatever fight divided Kentucky Presbyterians. The son of John Breckinridge, a Jeffersonian of national stature, he first studied law while he managed his mother's estate.[22] He became a member of the Kentucky legislature in 1825 (defeated in an election in 1829), a trustee of Transylvania University, and an opponent of "Sabbath mail delivery." During the late 1820s, Breckinridge had an intense personal religious experience which led to his joining the Presbyterian Church, perhaps caused in part by grief at the death of two children and by his own serious illness. Within months he became Ruling Elder in the Mt. Horeb Church, located on his farm.[23]

Elected a lay representative to the General Assemblies of 1831 and 1832 by the Presbytery of West Lexington, Breckinridge joined an assault on the thirty-year-old tradition of allowing members of the Congregationalist branch of American Calvinism to sit on committees of the

Presbyterian General Assembly.[24] He evidently read voraciously in areas of theology, for when he applied for ministerial candidacy (September 1831), and a license to preach (April 1832), West Lexington Presbytery sustained the examinations. He studied for a few months at Princeton Seminary, and in June 1832, he accepted the call to become minister of the Second Presbyterian Church in Baltimore.[25]

Like Nathan Rice, Breckinridge attacked Catholics and received a libel suit for his vituperation. Unlike Rice, Breckinridge won his suit in 1840. And like Cleland, Breckinridge coalesced party sentiment in the split between Old and New Schools within Presbyterianism. While still in Baltimore, Breckinridge took on Universalists and distillers of whiskey, arguing that both undercut public needs for law and order.[26]

After a disastrous stint as President of Jefferson College, 1845–47, he returned to Kentucky to become pastor of the First Presbyterian Church in Lexington. In September 1847, he accepted a concurrent responsibility as Superintendent of Public Instruction for the State of Kentucky, a position he held until 1853.[27]

Breckinridge fought tooth and nail to get the state governmental structures to support public education with adequate funding. He overcame the opposition of Governor John Helm especially, and his efforts resulted in a vastly improved system of state aid for "Common Schools." He argued on another front that in time public schools should absorb parochial schools and that universal, basic education transmitted culture while it opened the whole citizenry to opportunities and responsibilities in the world. A measure of his success as the proponent of public education in Kentucky can be determined from the fact that enrollment of children in "common schools" increased from 20,602 in 1847 to 201,223 in 1853, and average attendance arose by a multiple of seven during those years.[28]

The issues of education, important as they were for Breckinridge, paled in comparison with the issues surrounding the institution of slavery. Again, with characteristic fervor, Breckinridge worked in behalf of his convictions. He considered slavery immoral and inefficient; he knew of its impact for he had received the "benefits" of slavery as he grew up at Cabell's Dale. When Breckinridge moved to become a minister, he pledged to set free the children of his slaves. Two years later, he freed some older slaves, and in 1835 he arranged a plan to free the rest over a period of years.[29]

He vociferously advocated a rather moderate, anti-slavery position which caused friction in the slaveowning portions of his family and which again helped divide the Presbyterian Church. But his leadership was so tied to the matter of slavery that to discuss his contribution is to discuss slavery in Kentucky Presbyterianism.

Slavery and Anti-slavery

Some Kentucky Presbyterians opposed slavery, while others defended it. Some freed their slaves as a result of religious conviction, while others received slaves and kept them out of ethical concern. Some Kentucky Presbyterians were slaves, others, ex-slaves. Taken as a whole, the picture regarding slavery among the Presbyterians began and continued to be a confusing one. Even during the frontier era, Kentucky Presbyterians had been on both sides of the question. As already indicated, David Rice had spearheaded anti-slavery attempts to bar the institution altogether. As that effort failed, he and some other leaders in the church had sought to provide for the gradual emancipation of blacks.[30] The Kentucky Abolition Society, founded in 1808, continued in the tradition Rice had begun. Frequently overlooked in consideration of slavery is the fact that numbers of families kept moving to Indiana and Ohio because they disapproved of slaveowning.

In time, the wealth of the minority of Kentucky Presbyterians who owned slaves increased. Simultaneously the efforts in behalf of emancipation became more organized. Some slaveowners sought to educate their charges. Evidence also exists that some of the anti-slavery forces organized attempts to secure the manumission of individuals.

Overall, slaveowning thoroughly permeated Kentucky Presbyterianism. Doubtless some congregations existed throughout the period with no slaveowning members, but analysis of eighteen congregations thus far has not confirmed one. Historian Lowell Harrison says that of 139,920 white families listed in the 1850 census, 28% held slaves, although very few held over 100 slaves. Typically, a slaveowning family held only a few, and family wills provided for disposition of the slaves within the same family.[31]

Investigation of slaveowning in Shelby County, Kentucky, for example, shows that of the five elders thought to be the first ordained in the church, all held slaves at the time of their deaths.[32] The will of one of three elders active in 1833 provides for disposition of slaves.[33] All five located wills of early deacons show that those men held slaves.[34] Elder Robert Allen in 1834 specified that two of his eight slaves be freed at the death of his wife, and he made provision for the more distant freedom of all.[35] Elder Singletary Wilson said "I have held these notes to save the Negroes," and bound one (Godfrey) to James Hickman to become a blacksmith so his wages could also sustain another (John) who was blind."[36]

Lexington Presbyterians appear to have been equally immersed in slaveowning, although records are not as readily available.

First Presbyterian Church records relating to antebellum years are not now available, but from materials pieced together, one researcher has quilted a list of officers which numbers nineteen. Only five of their wills can be located, but four of the five men had owned slaves. Only John Maxwell appears to have left no slaves when he died in 1819.[37]

All the others—John McDowell, David Logan, Robert Patterson and William Allen—apparently possessed more than one slave apiece. Allen evidently owned at least two;[38] Patterson, four;[39] Logan, five;[40] and McDowell, nine.[41] At McDowell's death the certified trustees in 1840 valued his rifle at $9.25, all his combined property at about $5,000. Almost exactly half the total of his estate consisted in the slaves, two of whom only accounted for $20 of that amount—"Darcy," an "old woman," and "Henry," "old man." Ben, however, was appraised at $850; Aaron, at $920. Logan's will, the most blatantly theological of the lot, may have served equally as a suicide note. "Having lived long enough on this sinful world," Logan said, he had "no one but myself to blame for this rash deed." He lamented that his son "Joseph has no more interest in land or negroes [sic] than [did] either of the girls. . . . " Logan in 1858 left one "old woman" of "no value," three man slaves, and a "Boy, diseased."[42]

Slaveowning in Louisville and in nearby Oldham County was widespread, too. In Bourbon County fewer than half the session members from early years had wills in that county's probate system before the Civil War. But evidently a majority of them held no slaves. Joseph Mitchell, one of the few who died with a slave showing on his inventory, specified that "my negro [sic] woman Amy, shall be free from me and my heirs forever."[43]

One glimpse into the ambiguous nature of slavery in Kentucky is afforded by examination of the ministry of John Rankin at the Concord and Cane Ridge Churches, 1817–1821. Rankin, who had already made known his anti-slavery sentiments as a student at Samuel Doak's academy in Tennessee, moved through Kentucky on his way to Ohio. He planned to settle there because it offered freedom for blacks, but a lame horse forced Rankin to delay in the Bluegrass area.[45]

Presbyterians at the Cane Ridge and Concord Churches needed a minister. When Rankin served as a satisfactory interim, they invited him to stay among them. John Rankin and his family purchased a few acres and built a house on the land while he received ordination from Ebenezer Presbytery and served as pastor for the two churches.[46]

Rankin noted that the Concord (Bourbon County) and Cane Ridge congregations possessed only one slaveowner between them. One of the founders of the Concord Church, Samuel Donnell, also led the Carlisle branch of the Kentucky Abolition Society. Eight years before Rankin arrived to lead them, the session of the Concord Church had excluded a slaveowner from membership who offered a young man for sale at public auction.[47]

The two congregations gave emotional support to all of Rankin's efforts to end slavery. They helped him teach slaves to read in the school Rankin started. They sustained in session and congregational vote a resolution to exclude slaveowners from membership, and they allowed him to preach widely on the subject—in Cynthiana, Maysville, Flemingsburg, and Augusta. Ironically, so many members of the churches were opposed to slavery to such extent that they moved to Indiana and Ohio, leaving Rankin's salary in arrears. Their lack of financial support led the indebted minister to sell his property and to move to Ripley, Ohio, where he pursued his abolitionism fiercely until all American slaves were freed.[48]

It should be noted that while a majority of members of the Presbyterian churches at Concord and Cane Ridge opposed slavery, a majority of the residents in the Carlisle area opposed Rankin. They threatened his life; they mobbed his school; they beat and assaulted the slaves he taught. Nor would Ebenezer Presbytery in 1817–21 allow one of its congregations to make such exclusions as Rankin's churches sought to do. The court would only urge slaveowners to train their slaves and take them to worship. Rankin, in disappointment and desperation, managed to host those of similar anti-slavery persuasion one more time—as the Kentucky Abolition Society met at Concord Church in October, 1821—and then he left the state.[49]

The specifics of slavery among Kentucky Presbyterians accentuate the ambiguity slavery afforded. On the one hand, slaves were valuable; on the other, provision for the old and infirm among the slaves proved costly. On the one hand, Presbyterians generally recognized the evil of the institution; on the other they were reluctant to deprive their families, or themselves, by emancipating those they owned. Although few Kentuckians arrived at the later southern position alleging the superiority of slavery over a free society, some did justify the owning of slaves on biblical grounds.

The judicatories generally became less eager to address the issue of slavery as time elapsed. In 1833, the Synod voted (41–36 with 1 abstention) that "it is inexpedient to come to any decision on the very difficult and delicate question of Slavery, as it exists within our bounds, therefore Resolved that the whole subject be indefinitely postponed."[50]

At the very next meeting, however, Synod adopted (56–8, with 7 abstaining) a condemnation of the institution in principle and the beginning of a plan to end it. Such a forceful statement, appearing when it did, is worthy of notice:

> This Synod, believing that the system of absolute and hereditary domestic slavery, as it exists among the members of our communion, is repugnant to the principles of our holy religion, as recorded in the sacred scriptures, and that the continuance of the system, any longer than is necessary to prepare for its safe and beneficial termination is sinful, feel it their duty earnestly to recommend to all Presbyteries, Church Sessions, and people under their care, to commence immediate preparation for the termination of slavery among us. . . .[51]

Synod resolved to charge a committee with the preparation of a plan which could be implemented in the churches, named the committee, and endorsed the "scheme of African Colonization" which would be "an act of justice to the unfortunate African race among us, and for spreading the blessings of civilization and the everlasting gospel in the interior of Africa."[52]

For most of the antebellum period in Kentucky, the majority of plans for emancipation, including the one that Synod endorsed, involved "colonization." The American Colonization Society (ACS) had been formed in 1816, conceived by Presbyterian Robert Finley and patterned on the English experiment in Sierra Leone. Either free blacks or slaves conditionally freed would be "returned to Africa" to civilize and evangelize the "Dark Continent." The removal of blacks from the U.S. would also give hope to slaves, and a "white America" would be the result.[53]

Kentuckian Henry Clay, and other Americans of national reputation, served as presidents of the ACS. The strategy for implementation of the plan skillfully mixed governmental and voluntary resources. The General Assembly of 1818 denounced slavery and supported colonization.[54] The Synod of Kentucky in 1823 was just one of the judicatories that expressed approval of it. Presbyterian papers, the *Western Luminary* and the *Presbyterian Herald* among them, published articles advocating colonization. By 1830, the *African Repository*, the official organ of the ACS said: "Probably in no state of the Union has the scheme of African Colonization found more decided friends or met with more general approbation than in Kentucky."[55]

A primary leader of the Kentucky Colonization Society for most of its life, Robert Breckinridge accentuated the need for it to concentrate upon the emancipation of black people. John C. Young, the President of Centre; John A. McClung, sometime historian and lawyer; James G. Birney, the Kentuckian returned from slave owning in Alabama; Thomas Skillman, the publisher; William Breckinridge, Robert's brother; and a score of other prominent Presbyterians stayed in the forefront of the society for at least a portion of the period.[56]

Though the Colonization Society proved the most popular antislavery organization during the border period, it produced few tangible results. Leaders in the voluntary sector could not influence legislators to enact a tax on slaves by which slaveowners might pay the considerable costs of implementation. The few Kentucky black people who journeyed to Liberia did not recommend it highly for sisters and brothers. More important, many free blacks in seaboard cities frequently let it be known they considered the scheme a plot to make America "white" by attrition if not genocide of blacks. These negative results, together with the general unwillingness of slaveowners to manumit slaves, made the "Colonization Plan" a discouraging alternative.[57]

More straightforward anti-slavery efforts drew less popular support. The Kentucky Abolition Society, formed in 1808 largely by evangelical Christians including Presbyterians, never attracted many members. Its views reached the public, however, when in 1822 the pastor of the Presbyterian Church at Shelbyville, John Finley Crowe, published the *Abolition Intelligence and Missionary Magazine*. He devoted eight full pages each month for two years to the plans in various areas of the country, including his own. When Crowe moved to Indiana a year later, no one picked up the responsibility for its appearance.[58]

After the nature of abolitionism changed to demand immediate, uncompensated emancipation, certainly by 1835, Kentucky Presbyterians still formed the nucleus of an anti-slavery movement which focused on the constitutional convention of 1849. William L. Breckinridge gave the main address to a Louisville rally of emancipationists in February 1849. Robert Breckinridge framed the motion at the April convention of the party in Frankfort: the new constitution would specify ways to ameliorate the conditions of slaves and to end the institution. Thirteen of the twenty-one ministers who served as delegates to the convention were Presbyterians. Many lay leaders in the Reformed bodies also came. When the election for delegates to the Constitutional Convention occurred, the pro-slavery forces won overwhelmingly, though, and destroyed any possibility that Kentucky would move by law to become a free state.[59]

Two native Kentuckians stand out as later Presbyterian advocates of anti-slavery—James G. Birney and John G. Fee. Birney, born in Danville, heard Rice and other anti-slavery Kentucky Presbyterians as he grew up. Pro-slavery in his views, Birney studied law, served in the state legislature, and owned slaves himself. Moving to Alabama to plant cotton in 1818, Birney took his slaves and secured more. Financial reverses made him sell the plantation and the field slaves; subsequent prosperity in law practice at Huntsville gave Birney some leisure to engage in voluntary philanthropy. He became an agent for the American Colonization Society, serving five southern states.[60]

In 1833, he moved back to Danville convinced that slavery was both morally corrupt and economically inefficient. Birney started his own voluntary society dedicated to convincing slaveowners to free their human property, while he still worked with the Kentucky Colonization

Society. He debated John C. Young as he moved to consider immediate manumission as the only alternative. Birney led in the forming of a new Kentucky Anti-Slavery Society, with immediate emancipation as its avowed goal. Birney planned to publish a paper, but mass meetings and threats against potential printers kept him from the project. Birney himself was forced to move to Cincinnati to continue the fight which by now consumed his energies.[61]

John G. Fee, born in Bracken County, had gone north to Lane Seminary for theological education. Returning in 1842 to his slaveowning family, he announced that he considered the institution of slavery evil and that he would work for its demise. He received ordination in the New School and began to pastor small congregations in Lewis and Bracken Counties. He also married Matilda Hamilton, a young woman of similar abolitionist convictions, in 1844. His congregations would allow no slaveowners to partake in communion, a stance which forced him from the New School and into a Baptist ecclesiology.[62] He also found theological reasons for denominational shift. Where Birney remained a Presbyterian and moved to Ohio, Fee moved to an independent church position and tried to remain in Kentucky. With Matilda and a few other families, he moved in 1854 to Madison County to found "Berea" on land donated by Cassius M. Clay, who sought political power in that area. Berea College, open to blacks and white alike, opened in 1858 amid fierce opposition from what Fee termed "the Slave power." The school and symbiotic churches suffered a precarious existence, but offered a radical alternative to Kentucky slavery and the condoning of slaveowning.[63]

Fee, between 1842 and 1845 a Kentucky New School Presbyterian, represented yet another area of contention in antebellum Kentucky Presbyterianism. The Old School/New School battle, inextricably bound to the slavery-anti-slavery issue, consumed much Presbyterian energy and activity during the period.

Old and New Schools

On a national scale, resentment among many Presbyterians grew in the face of perceived theological innovations on the part of New Englanders Nathaniel Taylor and Samuel Hopkins. The doctrines of sin, human depravity, human ability, and others were receiving expression that differed from the Westminster Standards. Whether they also differed from the teachings of the Bible, the authority for faith and practice according to the Standards, or whether they called Christians into a new interpretation of what the Standards taught in light of the Bible depended upon one's point of view.

Hopkins, for example, had been an intimate associate of Jonathan Edwards and was deeply influenced by Edwards' concentration on original sin. Like Edwards, he attempted to address the question, "Why was sin in the world?" Hopkins wrote a systematic theology that encouraged people to practice "disinterested benevolence." "Disinterested benevolence is pleased with the public interest, the greatest good and happiness of the whole. This is the highest good to the benevolent person." Affection (a synonym for benevolence) which is selfless follows the example of Jesus Christ, the obligation of the redeemed person. "Jesus Christ is a remarkable and striking instance of disinterested benevolence, in which Christians are to imitate him."[64]

Hopkins himself illustrated the manner in which this affection should be directed. He wrote early in a forceful fashion against the institution of slavery. In a dialogue first published in 1776, Hopkins had pointed out the irony of American struggles to gain independence so that black people could be oppressed in slavery. He likewise linked antislavery sentiments with other reform needs, such as temperance and impiety. Later he continued his attack on the system of chattel slavery, asking after quoting the words of prophets and apostles, "How can we attend to the voice of God in these sacred writings, and not see that you (slaveowners) are most clearly pointed out? And will you not be affronted, or even disregard us, while we entreat and conjure you by all that is important and sacred, so far as to regard these threatenings and promises, and pursue your own highest interest and that of the public, as to let your oppressed slaves go out free?"[65] It was this focus upon God's goodness, human movement to expel evil, and the explicitness of the evils (especially slavery) which provoked a reaction both pro and con in the church.

Proponents of Hopkinsianism praised the simplicity of the system and the consonance of Calvinism with reform endeavor and revival techniques. Opponents of the theology cited its departures from the Calvinism of the Standards, and increasingly a rigid, American expression of the Westminster perspectives began to form. The movement in reaction to Hopkins, and to Taylor also, gradually came to center at Princeton Seminary. The "Princeton Theology" accused followers of Hopkins and Taylor of being Arminian and Pelagian in their doctrines of sin, redemption, and grace.[66]

One mainstay of the growing "Old School" in Presbyterianism, Charles Hodge, served notice from the very first of his professorship at Princeton—he would broach no theological innovations departing from traditional Calvinism. In his introductory lecture, he claimed forcefully, "The Armenian [sic] system is the natural expression of feelings less strongly marked, of less reverence for God, less humiliating views of man, and in general of less prominence and depth of religious character." Persons who depart from Calvinism in this direction have "no inward necessity for the doctrines of the gospel, no apprehension of God's holiness, no fear of his justice, no adequate sense of sin, need no atoning Savior, and no sanctifying Spirit. . . . "[67]

To question the theology of the Westminster Standards for Old School Presbyterians meant to doubt the very message of the Bible itself. Again, where the New School concentrated on reform through cooperative and voluntary structures, the Old School worked through denominational channels for most reform efforts that seemed to them consistent with the theology of Westminster. Doctrinal theology mixed thoroughly with the politics and sectional alliances of the Presbyterians.

New School Presbyterians, following the direction provided by Hopkins in his "disinterested benevolence" as the desired goal of Christian life, sought all kinds of ways to improve the human condition by reforming persons and institutions wherever they could. Yale, Andover, Auburn, and Union— centers for New School theology in the East— were also places where the reform movement flourished. Princeton, and its related educational offspring on the "Log College" model, harbored less of the interdenominatinal and interrelated reforms, particularly anti-slaveryism. Therefore, Princeton was seen as being sympathetic with the South and its peculiar institution.[68]

Anti-slavery sentiment proved just one, albeit focal, reform. Also included in the cluster of issues were temperance, peace, women's rights, child labor, and even the development of city parks. Many leaders in behalf of these issues sought interdenominational missionary activity, dissemination of Christian doctrines, and free access to the Holy Bible. The American Home Mission Society, the American Tract Society, and the American Bible Society were developed to meet these needs. With some of the reform associations, New School Presbyterians represented a "right wing" if they did not outright repudiate them—as in the movement for women's rights and peace. In others, such as the American Bible Society, Old School Presbyterians joined, and even led, portions of the voluntary associations. On still other reforms, the cessation of Sunday mail delivery or temperance, for example, "Schools" apparently mattered not a whit. Nor does one branch or Presbyterianism stand out in its "nativism" (particularly the anti-Catholic agitation that plagued American Protestantism, masquerading as yet another reform). By and large, however, the New School Presbyterians energized the reforms, while many Old School Presbyterians considered most of the same movements of questionable merit in light of human depravity. And Old Schoolers termed much of anti-slavery and women's rights outright demonic.[69]

Naturally most Kentucky Presbyterians who had not broken (or been broken) from the Synod in Stoneite and Cumberland splits were Old School in their allegiances. Many of those who might have been susceptible to New School influences no longer participated in the Synod. They were now Cumberland Presbyterians, or Disciples of Christ or they had moved north toward a more compatible Presbyterianism.

Still, there appears to have been little in the way of tension on the matter of benevolent societies within the Synod of Kentucky until the 1830s. Animosity arose gradually, especially toward the American Home Missionary Society, the primary vehicle for New Schoolers. The Synod of 1827 heard Thomas Cleland preach a missionary sermon and then took up a collection of $105.50 after he finished speaking. The money was specifically for "the use and benefit of the American Home Missionary Society of New York."[70] Synod that same year took formal action on a recommendation to "cooperate with their brethren of every denomination, together with every other friend of humanity, in one great national effort to accomplish a universal change in the habits and customs of our country relative to the intemperate use of ardent spirits." Synod "embraced" the proceedings of the General Assembly on the matter—likewise those of the American Society for the Promotion of Temperance. Synod "warmly recommended" to member congregations the work of the Rev. David Blythe, an agent of the American Bible Society. Thus they acted in approbation of the benevolent societies at every turn during their meeting that year.[71]

The following year, 1828, saw the Synod listening to the Episcopalian advocate of colonization, Benjamin O. Peers, an agent for the American Colonization Society.[72] They afterward responded to his address with a resolve to "view with deep interest the efforts of the American Colonization Society and (Synod) warmly recommend(s) to the people under their care, as far as they have it in their power, to promote its benevolent and philanthropic objects." More than a token, $715.75 was subscribed to the effort—$97.75 paid on the spot.[73] Again that year, the American Bible Society was "encouraged" in its efforts, but a proposition to seek "advancement of the gradual emancipation of the people of colour of this state" was tabled.

As late as 1829, at least one of the constituent presbyteries, Transylvania, was still requesting the services of a full-time missionary among them from the American Home Missionary Society. The presbytery itself was willing to pay half the expenses, if the minister would work in Manchester, Barbourville, and London.[74]

But in that same year, Muhlenburg Presbytery in western Kentucky offered a Minute expressing "gratefulness" to the Board of Missions of the General Assembly for sending a missionary to labor among them. The resolution said they approved of the source of this missionary—a denominational board—and "feel bound to sustain it by our prayers and influence. . . . " Only two years earlier, that same presbytery had commissioned member William Stewart to "correspond with the Director, Home Missionary Society and to state to them our wants. . . . " Thus sentiment had begun to swing away from the American Home Missionary Society by the turn of the decade.[75]

In 1830 matters appear to have become more pointed with regard to benevolent societies. The American Bible Society received words of praise from Synod, and Synod still heard from representatives of the American Colonization Society and the American Society for Promotion of Temperance. Even the American Board of Commissioners for Foreign Missions was a recipient of funds. But the American Home Missionary Society received neither praise nor "floor-time."[76]

The following year, 1831, saw Synod passing a series of resolutions on the subject of voluntary societies and missions. It was evidently directed at the American Home Missionary Society in particular. Action stated approval of connectional government, disagreement with any plan to cooperate in domestic missions that was not totally accountable to the General Assembly, and determination to send representatives to a conference on "Missions in the Valley of the Mississippi" dedicated to this point of views. It was the preamble to the resolutions that accused the American Home Missionary Society of abusing its power, of being unresponsive to the people. The lengthy preface warned that only a revolution would suffice to overthrow the power of the voluntary societies, since they had no "checks and balances" built into their structures (as did the courts of Presbyterianism).[77]

The document is noteworthy also for its naive and thorough-going identification of the Christian church (especially Presbyterianism) with the American governmental structure. Washington's words of warning about the future threats to the U.S. were simply quoted, substituting "church" for "government." At one point, rhetoric became even more grandiose: "The history of the world affords sufficient proof that Republics have become corrupt and then the *people* were not safe depositories of power. Shall we therefore abandon our republican institutions and bestow the power of government on a few—a society, a king. . . . "[78]

In 1833 the Synod of Kentucky again repudiated the American Home Missionary Society. But Kentucky Presbyterians took pains to affirm on pragmatic grounds the American Tract Society and the American Bible Society. Kentucky Presbyterians likewise found reason to rally around the statements of the Old School sentiments and statements of frustration after the General Assembly of 1834 gathered in the "Act and Testimony" which Robert J. Breckinridge drafted. The Act and Testimony articulated some "alarming errors which have hitherto been connived at, and now at length have been countenanced and sustained" by the General Assembly. Specifically, the statement complained that new interpretations of authoritative doctrines were departing from and subverting the traditions. The "errors" named were seven characterizations (or caricatures) of New School theology. Heretics believed, for example, "that we have no more to do with the first sin of Adam than with the sins of any other parent," "that there is no such thing as original sin," and "that Christ's sufferings were not truly and properly vicarious." Errors, in addition, existed in matters of "Imputation," "Ability," "Regeneration," and "Divine Influence." The complainants sought "speedy remedy" of the situation, lest theological seminaries "be converted into nurseries to foster the noxious errors."[79]

The Synod of Kentucky, meeting in Danville in October, 1834, approved in formal fashion the doctrinal part of the "Act. . . . " They also adopted several resolutions which pertained to the document, statements presented by James Stonestreet, an elder from West Lexington Presbytery, who urged that ministers or elders "holding these errors . . . should be arraigned before the proper tribunal without delay." Another resolution dealt with the rights of presbyteries to "judge of the qualifications of its own members;" another, with the alleged violation of the Presbyterian Constitution in any appointment of "mutual councils" or "commmitteemen." In all, the votes were resoundingly favorable to the cause of Old School Presbyterianism.[80]

That same year Kentucky's own Joshua L. Wilson, who served just across the river in Cincinnati's First Presbyterian Church, accused the famed Lyman Beecher of heresy. Beecher had come from eastern Congregationalism four years earlier at the invitation of Wilson (and other members of the Board of Directors) to head the new Lane Seminary. Perhaps the fact that Beecher also undertook to pastor the Second Presbyterian Church of Cincinnati chafed Wilson and caused his action. Maybe it was the increasing self-consciousness of the Old School, to which Wilson wholeheartedly belonged. It could have been simply a case of growing personal disaffection, or other reasons that Wilson could have brought charges. Whatever the precipitating causes, the heresy trial of Beecher became a point of local Presbyterian interest and identification in the midst of national party strife. Kentucky followed faithfully the proceedings in Ohio against the New Schooler Beecher.[81]

By the time Synod met in the fall of 1836, the militancy of an Old School majority within the state predominated almost entirely. A series of resolutions formally expressed the feelings of most in no uncertain terms: one took Wilson's side in the controversy with Beecher, stating that "the language employed in our public standards in its plain and obvious meaning does most explicitly set forth the doctrines and principles of the Presbyterian Church;'' another took the side of the complainants against New Schooler Albert Barnes, being tried for his theology as set forth in a biblical commentary. ''*The Notes on Romans* . . . is an unsound and dangerous book.'' Still other resolutions expressed ''deep regret'' that the General Assembly of 1836 had failed to support the Western and Foreign Missionary Society as well as ''hope'' that the following Assembly would reverse the course of action. Companion resolutions declared opposition to any ''further operation of the American Home Missionary Society and American Education Society'' within Synod bounds, and ''required'' these organizations to ''retire without delay'' from their work in Kentucky. Feeble protests were presented by eleven of the members of Synod against these resolutions, representing about 20 percent of the assembled body.[82]

When the split finally did occur, and the General Assembly of 1837 managed with its Old School majority to abrogate the Plan of Union, to dissolve the synods formed under its auspices, and to cease involvement institutionally in the interdenominational societies that fostered ''New Schoolism,'' Kentucky Presbyterians followed suit with resolutions endorsing these actions in their own meeting of Synod that fall.[83] The Synod of Kentucky met a full four months after the General Assembly. A ''Committee on Minutes of the General Assembly'' presented its report which soon became the ''order of the day.'' A minority report to the Synod was simultaneously tabled. According to the report itself, adopted as amended, the Synod concurred with General Assembly in calling into question the Plans of Union of 1801 and 1808. The vote showed 70 favoring the Old School motion, 20 opposed, and 5 abstaining. A second resolution judged the plans abrogated, by a larger margin. The vote proved still more than 2–1 when it came to the upholding of General Assembly actions to excind New School Synods. Similar affinities showed in the resolve to refuse admission to New School delegates for the upcoming 1838 Assembly.[84]

It is interesting to observe that the same meeting of Synod resolved to encourage both the American Bible Society and the American Tract Society in their work. The Synod evidently wanted to assure leaders of, and believers in, these voluntary organizations that they would not repudiate efforts of the entire benevolent enterprise in this Old School movement.[85]

The General Assembly of 1838, with Old Schoolers from Kentucky and the rest of the Synods firm in their commitment to follow the direction of the previous year, refused admission to ministers and elders from excinded New School courts. New School elders and clergy then moved down the street to form their own Assembly. When the Synod of Kentucky acted subsequently to ratify membership in the Old School, several of the reluctant withheld approbation of the ''Reforming measures'' of the Assemblies of '37 and '38. Some agreement, either tacit or explicit, gave these ministers and elders assurance there would be no gloating or partisanship displayed by members of the Synod.[86]

Two powerful Old School proponents did speak out, however, and helped disrupt the tenuous unity the Synod enjoyed. They helped precipitate withdrawal of sympathizers of the New School from Synod. Nathan L. Rice wrote a parochial piece for the *Protestant and Herald*, and Robert J. Breckinridge endorsed the article with an editorial. The paper from Bardstown was a private venture and not an official Synod organ. But those leaning toward the New School anyhow perceived, perhaps justly, that Old Schoolers would not compromise their voices when political victory was assured. They began to leave.[87]

Meanwhile, as recent research by Harold Parker has indicated, a New School pastor was called by the Presbyterian Church in Bowling Green. The Reverend Archer C. Dickerson was called in 1839 and Old School members of Muhlenburg Presbytery, to which Bowling Green belonged, sought to block the entrance of Dickerson into the church. The church reacted by receiving Dickerson as its interim pastor. They also elected a full slate of officers entirely sympathetic to the positions of the New School. The congregation and its session, with Dickerson as pastor, moved to excise Old Schoolers from membership and to become the first New School Presbyterian Church in Kentucky, in January 1840.[88]

Simultaneously, Woodford County Presbyterians were listening to Joseph C. Stiles denounce Old Schoolism in favor of the New School, answering the allegations made by Rice and Breckinridge. His Presbytery of West Lexington proceeded quickly to warn Stiles to be more circumspect in his expressions. Rather than capitulate, Stiles called a convention in Versailles of those inclined toward the New School. It met in March 1840, and Dickerson attended, as did another New School pastor,

Alexander W. Campbell, and several elders. In all, 29 persons were present.[89]

A New School Presbytery did not form until December 1840, at the impetus of Dickerson and Stiles. West Lexington Presbytery had just found Stiles guilty of contumacy and relieved him of his ministerial responsibilities. He, in turn, relieved the presbytery of several congregations or parts of them. When the "Presbytery of Kentucky," (New School) met in Lexington on December 19, 1840, they sought to form a Synod of their own, with three presbyteries called "Green River," "Harmony," and "Providence." Each presbytery possessed a minimum of clergy (3) at the beginning.[90] What they lacked in numbers, they recovered in rhetoric. They declared themselves a church body "to preserve unimpaired the integrity of the Constitution of the Presbyterian Church." One scholar suggests that the Synod of Kentucky (New School) at first resisted identification with the appropriate General Assembly because already by 1840 that New School Assembly represented anti-slavery sentiments. At any rate, the final joining of the new Synod of Kentucky to the new General Assembly occurred in 1843.[91]

Leadership in the new Synod of Kentucky rested in the powers of Stiles, Dickerson, and Thomas Cleland. As previously explored, Cleland had sensed his calling amid the creative confusion of the early camp-meetings. For years he had served the New Providence Church and his reputation as a preacher and minister was perhaps the most lofty of any of the Kentucky clergy. His parting from the Old School grieved even the most belligerant partisan. Most members of the New Providence Church apparently followed Cleland in the realignment.[92]

Stiles, at once more contentious and more eccentric than Cleland, centered the affections of many Woodford Countians in the New School, but he moved to Richmond, Virginia in 1844, shortly after the Synod became affiliated with the New School General Assembly. By one account, Stiles had all the characteristics of the winsome persuader—"a perfect torrent of eloquence," as well as "fluency, animation, and zeal."[93]

Dickerson, third leader of the Synod, had come originally from Campell County via Miami (Ohio) University and a pastorate in Mississippi. He managed to accommodate congregations in Bowling Green so that cooperative use of the same buildings occurred for years between the competitive congregations of New and Old School Presbyterians in Bowling Green.

New School Presbyterians never had an easy time in Kentucky. They numbered scarcely more than a thousand at any time. They sought to establish a seminary to train ministers locally, for those candidates they secured left for more agreeable environments nearer seminaries they attended elsewhere. William M. King, pastor of the Macedonia Presbyterian Church in Woodford County, tried to arrange his schedule to spend part-time doing theological education. The attempt failed, however, for lack of funds.[94] Disappointment also came from the lack of support from the American Home Missionary Society, who could not successfully keep missionaries in Kentucky even when they turned their attention to the needs of the border state. Finally, in 1857, the Synod collapsed. Its failure may have come from the dearth of leadership—none arose to take the place of Stiles who left, or Cleland who died in that year. Perhaps, too, the New School got little support because Presbyterians depended on slavery, and the Old School offered a more hospitable climate for slaveowners and those connected with them. For whatever reason, the Synod fell apart about the time the New School split into Southern and Northern components over the matter of slavery.[95]

By comparison, the Old School in Kentucky fared very well. Congregations grew, though not dramatically. New ministers arose to take the place of former leaders, and the life of Kentucky Presbyterians was seemingly set in a pattern that in large measure still prevails.

The Rev. Robert J. Breckinridge (1800–1871), leader of the PCUSA (Old School) Synod of Kentucky, Minister of First Presbyterian Church, Lexington, and Professor at Danville Theological Seminary.

The Rev. Stuart Robinson (1814–1881), Professor at Danville Seminary and Pastor of Second Presbyterian Church, Louisville. He led border Presbyterians who joined the PCUS after the Civil War.

CHAPTER 5.

Civil War

In 1860–61, national issues overshadowed parochial concerns for Kentucky Presbyterians, as for the U. S. population generally. The United States came apart at the seams, and Kentucky was one of the seams. As analysts point out, Kentucky Presbyterians, together with those Kentuckians belonging to other mainline communions, felt border loyalties intensely. They felt drawn into both camps as they developed. Sympathy in the state for the Federal government outweighed secessionist sentiments both before and during the Civil War.[1]

The Spring of 1860 brought home the prospect, then the reality, of a split in society and church more grave than previous ones. The Democratic Party split at that time, with Kentucky Presbyterian John C. Breckinridge the presidential nominee of the Southern wing. Abraham Lincoln became the Republican candidate for President on May 16th.[2]

Union and Strife

Although New Schoolers had divided sectionally in 1857, Old School Presbyterians thought they could maintain unity. The denomination numbered about 300,000 in 1860, with about a third of their members in the South. During May 1860, the very month of Lincoln's nomination, a General Assembly met, gathering with no visible rancor and with considerable cooperation. They concentrated on such matters as ministerial education, domestic and foreign missions, and whether stage plays and dancing were sins.[3]

By the time Confederate States began to secede, only two organizations of Presbyterians existed in Kentucky—the Synod of Kentucky (Old School) and the Cumberland Synod of Kentucky. As already mentioned, the New School Synod had ceased its activity in 1857, at the occasion of Southern New Schoolers forming their United Synod. Although several thousand Kentuckians were members of the Cumberland Church in 1860, their influence upon affairs of state did not approach that of the Old School Synod nor substantially affect the course of allegiance.[4] With about 11,500 members and 135 ministers in Kentucky in 1860, the Synod of Kentucky (Old School) represented perhaps the most significant force in all the state for union.[5]

Presbyterians in Kentucky managed to elect and send delegates from all six presbyteries to the 1861 meeting of the General Assembly, which convened on May 16th, a full month after the fall of Fort Sumpter.[6] It was at that General Assembly that the famous "Spring Resolutions" precipitated a walkout by Southern delegates. Gardiner Spring, longtime pastor of the Brick Presbyterian Church in New York, offered a petition that July 1st be a day of prayer for Presbyterians, seeking forgiveness of sin, offering thanks for God's blessing on the nation, and seeking divine guidance and blessing on national rulers. Finally, he asked the Assembly to implore God to restore peace. He minced no words, stating that the Assembly should resolve that "it is the duty of the ministry and churches . . . to do all in their power to promote and perpetuate the integrity of these United States, uphold and encourage the Federal Government." The Assembly's endorsement of these resolutions may have been, as critics asserted, a bowing to public pressure; but 130 favored it and only 89 opposed the resolutions. Southerners left the Assembly, and Kentuckians evidently remained.[7]

The Synod of Kentucky managed to meet in October, amid terrible confusion in the state. That court expressed its regret that the General Assembly had made its pronouncements, and they likewise "deplored" the schism that had resulted. Synod urged "great mutual forbearance," too late to aid in reconciliation of Old School Northerners and Southerners but perhaps in behalf of self-interest, where forbearance was in short supply.[8]

A quorum could not be counted for the scheduled meeting in 1862, with the war front so near. The remnant that gathered postponed its meeting until May 1863, when they hoped order would again prevail. Good attendance and attention to regular business characterized the meeting of that next Synod. The "Narrative of the State of Religion . . . " reported that people were coming faithfully to church, and in several areas "refreshing" revivals were occurring.[9]

A major controversy erupted during the October meeting of Synod. George Morrison, pastor of the Mt. Pleasant Presbyterian Church, complained that elders had asked his concurrence in firing him. In February 1862, the Confederate sympathies of the congregation had been "aroused" by Morrison's pro-Union stance. Not to be outflanked, Morrison had made off with the keys and records of the church. Confederates, temporarily in control of the area, had forced him to surrender both keys and records. When Union forces again overran the parish, Morrison had likewise used the might of military commander to regain his symbols of control.[10]

Morrison complained also that the congregation for the most part "treated him as though (he were) dead." The Presbytery, West Lexington, had inquired; the Southern party had prevailed at the hearing. Morrison objected to both the manner in which the meeting took place, and to the decision to dissolve his pastoral relationship with the congregation. He was going elsewhere sometime soon, he protested, but through proper channels and not through such an unconstitutional process. After hearing Morrison's lengthy argument, and the points of view among Presbytery representatives, Synod voted to sustain the appeal and enjoined the congregation to pay Morrison's salary; they likewise urged Morrison to find work elsewhere and to resign that pulpit.[11]

Actual warfare in Kentucky was comparatively rare, but confusion sometimes reigned. A glimpse of the effects of the war on Presbyterian worship had been offered by Lizzie Hardin, a young woman who visited near Harrodsburg during the summer of 1862. The step-daughter of a Methodist minister, she possessed the presence of mind to write her impressions of what she considered "Union occupation":

> Though politics were not preached at any church in town yet Jimmie and I refused to go again to the Methodist Church because the preacher was a Union man. On our way to the Presbyterian Church we were told that

> they intended to arrest the ladies as the congregation came out. We went on however determined to risk the consequences. We found everything quiet and orderly as usual. At the opening prayer the minister remembered "those in distress" and came as near praying for the Secessionists as he dared. That was some comfort to us who like Dives, "lifted up our eyes in torment," and welcomed even a drop of water. The sermon had scarcely begun when the congregation were alarmed by the shouts and cries of the Home Guard in front of the church. Not knowing but that they had arrested others, Jimmie and I rushed out, each fearing for some relative. We found nothing however but a wagon load of soldiers who their work being done got drunk. . . . [12]

About a month later, after many rumors and reports, Lizzie Hardin heard for certain that Morgan's Raiders were coming. Again, she described the scene at the Presbyterian Church in Harrodsburg on that day as she raced there to find the niece of a friend: "The congregation was engaged in worship as though nothing were the matter. A group of Negro carriage drivers was before the door and they were pointing to each other where they could see the cavalry on the hill."[13]

Some few churches were actually damaged in the course of battles, such as the one in Perryville. Other church buildings were used by the army, as the one at Paris. Most frequently, though, in the words of Synod, congregations were merely "disturbed by the excitements growing out of the state of the Country."[14]

The disturbing of the churches was thorough and systemic. Descriptions of Louisville during War years, for example, portray pandemonium. The city and environs housed thousands of Federal forces, hundreds of Confederate prisoners, a Quartermaster's Corps for the Union Army, scores of store-fronts on Jefferson and Fifth devoted to "games of chance," the headquarters of the L&N, perhaps the most important link in the Union Supply route, and many other confusing elements of life.[15]

Fear reigned from time to time, as in July 1863, when Morgan's Raiders threatened the city. More serious, the uncoordinated guerilla raids by Confederates, brigands, and common criminals gave promise of anarchy. Louisvillians who still owned slaves in 1864 worried immensely that their property would be lost in enlistments of blacks for the Army. In April of that year, free blacks and slaves alike were forced to work on the series of forts built around the town in anticipation of further raids and insurrections. Blacks, of course, felt the frustration of not knowing their destiny and finding little they could do to affect it, an anxiety-producing situations of giant proportions.[16]

Breckinridge vs. Robinson

In personal terms, the nature of the border church can be seen in the contention between two ministers for its leadership and direction. Robert Breckinridge, already introduced as a controversialist advocating anti-slavery and Old School orthodoxy, sought to lead Kentucky Presbyterians into loyal Federal support and a continuation of Old School affiliation. Stuart Robinson on the other hand, tried to lead them in a neutral position during the Civil War and into the Southern Church afterward. These two ministers epitomized the struggle in several respects, both theologically and socially.

At the height of his power, Breckinridge commanded attention from all Kentuckians. But he did not necessarily convince them of the need to support the Union actively.[17]

Breckinridge, on the National Fast Day in January 1861, said in a Lexington speech that the duty of Kentucky was ''First. To stand by the Constitution and the Union of the country, to the last extremity. Second. To prevent, as for the moment the impending and immediate danger, all attempts to seduce her, all attempts to terrify her, into taking of any step inconsistent with her own constitution and laws. . . . '' His conclusion sought to stir the heart of Christian Kentucky to loyalty:

> After all, my friends, after all—we have the great promise of God that all things shall work together for good to them that love him. I do not know but that it might be the mind of God and his divine purpose to break this Union up, and to make of it other nations, that shall at last be more powerful than it, unitedly, would have been. . . . We have his divine assurance that all nations that have gone before us, and all that will follow us, and we ourselves, by our rise, by our progress, and alas! by our decay and ruin, are but instruments of his infinite purpose, and means in his adorable providence, whereby the everlasting reign of Messiah, the Christ of God, is to be made absolute and universal. . . .[18]

As he inaugurated the *Danville Quarterly Review* for Old School Presbyterians and anyone else who would read it, Breckinridge lamented the election of Lincoln and the secession of the six cotton states which had by that time (March 1961) withdrawn from the Union. His plea, "Our Country—Its Peril—Its Deliverance," advocated a way of peace and constitutional enforcement of the law. This approach, he argued, followed "the Word of God." "If we acknowledge the sacred Scriptures to be the divine rule of our faith and our practice, there ought to be an end to all extreme opinions, and all violent proceedings, on this entire subject."[19]

Stuart Robinson, fourteen years younger than Breckinridge, would not have argued against peace in principle or against attending to the Word of God. But he sought almost absolute neutrality of the church in matters social and political. Robinson knew Breckinridge well, but the two were unable to keep peace between themselves.

Born in Strabane, Tyrone County, Ireland, in 1814, Robinson emigrated as a child to the U. S., and grew up in the family of a minister in the Valley of Virginia. He graduated from Amherst and attended Union Seminary in Hampden Sidney, Virginia. In Greenbrier Presbytery, he served small mission churches until 1846. The congregation at Frankfort, Kentucky, then called him and Stuart Robinson quickly established himself as a community leader as well as a powerful preacher. After a brief pastorate in Baltimore, Robinson accepted the call by the Old School Assembly of 1856 to serve on the Danville Seminary faculty, teaching "church government and pastoral theology."[20]

Some of the substance of Robinson's teaching efforts can be gleaned from his book, *The Church of God as an Essential Element of the Gospel*. His doctrine of the church proved interesting in several respects. As a Calvinist he naturally perceived the church in terms of God's covenantal relationship with people. Following in the tradition, he tied the nature of the church to both the Old and New Testaments and to the preservation of the "people of God" through all ages. Paying most attention to its Scotch heritage, Robinson bragged unabashedly about the superiority of this theology when it could be mixed with Presbyterian polity. He did concede that other denominations might finally have equal access to the throne of grace.[21]

Particularly did Robinson appraise optimistically the American prospect for the future of the church. God had freed the American church "from the civil domination which, by violence or seduction, silenced the martyr-voice of her Scotch mother. . . . "[22] Granted difficulties in the American milieu—that one could scarcely determine sheep from goats, wheat from tares, in a voluntary church—it gave promise of becoming a new source of inspiration and providential instrument in God's hands. He viewed the separation of church and state as consonant with their differing institutional responsibilities. The State, ordained by God the Father, provided for reasonable human intercourse; the church, formed by Jesus the Mediator, lived for the purpose of redeeming the elect of God. "They are the two great powers that be, and are ordained of God to serve two distinct ends in the great scheme devised for man as fallen." In the book, Robinson did not explicitly make his full statement on the "spirituality of the church," his belief that matters religious and those political could and should remain distinct, but he concluded the section on church and state with a reference to Jesus' command to "render to Caesar the things that are Caesar's distinct from rendering to God the things that are God's. . . . "[23]

From the very beginning of his Danville days, Robinson locked horns with Breckinridge. Their combat probably resulted in part from their similarities in personality—both men were long on dedication and certain of their points of view, both short on tolerance of divergent views and open-mindedness. In Presbyterian vernacular, neither was particularly adept at "subjecting himself to his brethren in the Lord."[24] But theological differences also marked their fray. Robinson argued the spirituality of the church; Breckinridge considered its responsibility in all aspects of human life.[25] Students received both the blessing and the curse of their contention, both growing in their faith as they observed differences within the faculty and likewise learning little about Christian community or harmony of the church.

Tensions in the school dissipated somewhat when Robinson accepted the call of the Second Presbyterian Church in Louisville to become its regular pastor. In the summer of 1858, the family moved the seventy-five miles to Louisville, and Robinson undertook his new responsibilities. But Kentucky's status as a border state did not permit him a tranquil environment for developing the implications of his theology of "spirituality."[26]

After the Spring Resolutions passed, Robinson led Kentucky Presbyterians at the Synod which met shortly afterward in stating their dissent against the political interference of the Assembly in the affairs of government. It may have been the only occasion on which the two antagonists cooperated in a church endeavor. Their protest proved so vehement that the following General Assembly took exception to the minutes of the Synod.[27]

The war soon came even closer to the lives of Robinson and Breckinridge. Breckinridge monopolized the 1862 meeting of the Old School Assembly with his proposal that it adopt his paper "On the State of the Church and the Country." He also sought Assembly loyalty in his personal quarrel with Robinson, who accused Breckinridge of taking "advantage of the pulpit or theological chair as a politician." The Assembly voted overwhelming affirmation of Breckinridge's paper, which used strong language to declare that Church members must "uphold the Federal Government." It also affirmed his stance by asking that he withdraw his proffered resignation and continue as a seminary professor.[28]

Breckinridge's staunch Unionism took him into the Republican Party, and made him "Lincoln's chief counsellor and advisor in Kentucky," by one appraisal.[29] When the Republicans met in 1864 to renominate Lincoln, Breckinridge led the Kentucky delegation and served as temporary chairman of the convention.[30]

He maintained the Danville Seminary during the war, though its program shrank to a shadow of its former substance. He also saw members of his family, including nephew John C., move into places of responsibility and leadership in the Confederate cause. When the war ceased, he kept the pro-Federal stance that had marked his career. Breckinridge battled for Danville Seminary and Centre College to maintain their Old School identity, and he fought every attempt to undercut the power of the Federal government or the Assembly.[31]

After the 1862 Assembly, Robinson followed quite a divergent course. When he wrote about the action of that Assembly in his journal, called the *True Presbyterian*, federal troops evidently seized some copies of the number. Robinson himself, who traveled north to Canada to visit his invalid brother, was obliged to remain in Toronto for the duration of the war. Friends warned him that should he return to Louisville, he might be incarcerated for sedition. The *True Presbyterian* continued publication until 1864, under the editorship of Thomas Hoyt, a good friend of Robinson's.[32] In his absence as the pastor of Second Presbyterian, Robinson saw that services continued with John C. Young filling the pulpit most of the time. Robinson's wife Mary cared for the family in Louisville. Robinson himself spent his days in exile as a minister among Southern refugees in eastern Canada.

William Fleming, former student of Robinson's from Danville, then studying at the University in Toronto, rented a lecture hall and invited his mentor to begin preaching there on Sundays.[33] Weekly occasions on Sunday nights, similar in substance to Robinson's previous lectures and sermons in Frankfort and Louisville, also became increasingly popular with students and professionals in the city.[34] In his leisure from pastoral responsibilities, Robinson had the time to refine his discourses for publication. He published two books while in Canada—*Discourses of Redemption* which gave him much pleasure, and *Mosaic Slavery*, which brought some pain.

The book *Mosaic Slavery* came from Robinson's interpretation of the institution as the Hebrew people had practiced it.[35] He said that he felt obligated to treat the subject because the Bible treated it.[36] He may have said little about the present condition of slavery in the U. S. in 1865, but it was seen as a defense of the South's "peculiar institution," and Robinson throughout the rest of his life received notoriety for publishing it.[37]

Robinson's *Discourses of Redemption*, on the other hand, became a widely read and much-quoted book in the Presbyterian Church.[38] He waited until returning to Kentucky to have it printed.[39] In the work he followed John Calvin's argument that God used progressive revelation until the time of Jesus Christ when God's nature was fully disclosed. According to Robinson, Scripture truthfully describes this process and therein possesses a unique authority in the church. Since the writing of Scripture, the church had embodied testimony to the accuracy and inspiration of Scripture and to the plan of God's covenants which undergird it.[40]

Robinson's trauma did not end with the cessation of guns in the war. In a military court in Washington, D.C., he was accused of plotting against the Union with other Confederate sympathizers in Canada. According to witnesses Godfrey Hyams and Sandford Conover, Robinson helped to plan and support a conspiracy to transport clothes infected with yellow fever from the South to several Northern cities including Washington. Robinson considered that his personal enemy from Kentucky days, Attorney General James Speed, had instigated the trial. The proceedings received considerable publicity, despite the lack of proof and the "faulty character" of both government witnesses. No formal conviction resulted, but Robinson considered that his ministry was falsely compromised in the process.[41]

Stuart Robinson was completely exonerated and permitted to return freely to Louisville, but not before the alleged plot had been confused with another—the conspiracy to kill Lincoln. In Toronto Robinson was forced or chose to publish personally a pamphlet telling his side of the story. He had served in Canada only as a minister of the gospel. Yes, he had seen Hyams as a minister, helping what he thought to have been a beggar and his starving family. Yes, he had seen casually one Dr. Blackburn, who also had been accused of cooperating in the plot to send infected clothes northward. But Robinson had never seen or met John Wilkes Booth or any Colonel Steele, implicated in the assassination plot. Steele had never even been to Montreal, and Robinson had not been there in either 1864 or 1865, when the meetings allegedly took place.[42]

Robinson concluded his statement with a summary of his refutation of what he termed the "miserable fictions" generated by military authorities. He asserted that he had been and remained a loyal, taxpaying citizen of the U.S.[43]

When he returned to Louisville from exile in April 1866, Stuart Robinson was something of a hero to many Kentucky Presbyterians. Especially in Louisville Presbytery he was received as an embodiment of the border "martyr." Relations between the majority of that court and the Old School Assembly had been deteriorating during the course of the war years.

Declaration and Testimony

During the war, members of the Presbytery of Louisville (PCUSA) proved the most belligerent among the middle courts in the four border synods—Baltimore, Missouri, Upper Missouri, and Kentucky. The leadership in spirit of Stuart Robinson from Canadian exile, open hostility in many congregations between parties, the voice of Thomas Hoyt and subsequently of Samuel R. Wilson—all made the presbytery a hotbed of dissidence from 1861 onward. Hoyt, the pastor of First Presbyterian, Louisville, had been accused by Breckinridge of assisting Robinson in the conspiracy to undercut the professor's ministry. Wilson, who came to the Mulberry Church in Shelby County from New York, and who succeeded Hoyt at First in 1865, joined his voice as well to the frequent protests.[44]

When the Federal government invited Old School pastors licensed by the denomination's mission board to work in conquered Southern areas, Louisville Presbytery responded with a protest to that year's Assembly. The General Assembly not only turned down adoption of the protest, it made an "extended denunciation of slavery" instead.[45] In its 1865 sequel, the Old School went even further against the wishes of Hoyt, Wilson, Robinson and others by telling presbyteries to examine incoming ministers on their loyalty and anti-slavery orthodoxy. Since Kentucky law still permitted slavery (the Emancipation Proclamation had affected only "rebellious" states), such a pronouncement struck the majority in Louisville Presbytery as blatant church meddling in political affairs.[46]

In September 1865, the Louisville Presbytery adopted a *Declaration and Testimony against the Erroneous and Heretical Doctrines and Practices which have Obtained and been Propogated in the Presbyterian Church during the Last five years*. In a 27-page pamphlet, they published their grievances and statements of determination "to bring back the church of our fathers to her ancient purity and integrity, upon the foundation of the apostles and prophets, and under the banner of our only King."[47]

The argument consisted of three parts: a list of 14 "errors" in doctrine and practice; another list of six reasons to employ the word "error" of those fourteen points; and finally, a catalogue of ten resolutions. Among the "errors" cited were "the assumption of the courts of the church, of the right to decide questions of state policy," the belief "that the church as such owes allegiance to human rulers or governments" and "the action of the Assembly on the subject of slavery and emancipation in 1864, and confirmed in 1865." In addition, the *Declaration* . . . singled out the seminaries of Princeton and Danville, and their respective professors of theology, Hodge and Breckinridge, for special blame. Reasons for such a remonstrance about "errors" included beliefs that the church violated the Word of God and the doctrines of the Presbyterians, it "obliterated" the traditional distinction and separation between church and state, and brought ministers and churches into disrepute. The *Declaration* . . . accused the General Assembly of fomenting "strife and schism."[48]

Finally, the resolutions began with refusals: "to give support to ministers, elders, agents, editors, teachers . . . who hold the preceding [sic] or similar heresies," and "to take part in any discussion or decision" which pertained to matters of state. They would recognize only the written word of God as authority, they would take no oath, would support others adhering to these principles, cease to contribute to General Assembly boards, use their money to help those of like mind, and pray for restoration of the peace and purity of the church. In all, it was a thorough denunciation of the direcion taken by the General Assembly, ironically embodying the very vehicles of dissent that had given birth to the denomination as it then constituted itself.[49]

The Synod of Kentucky met in Louisville only one month after the action of the presbytery. Robert J. Breckinridge lost no time in pressing the attack against Louisville dissidents, presenting immediately a paper which questioned the rights of *Declaration and Testimony* . . . signers to sit in the court. He called on colleagues in the Synod to judge them "unqualified, unfit, and incompetent to sit and act" as members of the judicatory. Attempts to "table" or "refer" Breckinridge's paper failed, and it was docketed. Lengthy debate on the matter included readings from sources of Presbyterian authority—various actions of General Assemblies, the 22nd chapter of the *Confession of Faith*, many questions and answers from the Westminster Catechisms, and at least one chapter of Scripture, Matthew 22.[50]

Breckinridge finally lost, and a vote to seat ministers from Louisville Presbytery carried 4 to 1. But he and other leaders who desired a purge of the *Declaration* party from the body kept the matter before the marathon meeting of the Synod in anticipation of a reversal in a subsequent General Assembly. Fortunately for them, it tied nicely with the other major issue before the court—the sad history of the Walnut Street Presbyterian Church of Louisville. In addition, one member of Louisville Presbytery, the Reverend J. P. McMillan of Shelbyville, made a formal complaint against the presbytery, asking for redress. It would come, one way or another.[51]

Disaffected Presbyterians in Missouri and Maryland, together with scattered presbyters from various northern communities, signed the *Declaration and Testimony* . . . in the months following. Stuart Robinson, returning from Canadian exile, embodied defiance of the General Assembly request for statements of loyalty to the Federal Government. All the furor climaxed dramatically in the upcoming General Assembly of 1866, meeting in St. Louis.[52] Robinson was elected a representative from Louisville Presbytery as was Dr. Wilson, whom the dissidents nominated as Moderator. At the Assembly, Dr. R. L. Stanton of the Danville Seminary faculty and a close colleague of Breckinridge, was the nominee of those who sought to punish the protesters. Dr. Phineas D. Gurley, pastor of Washington's New York Avenue Presbyterian, where Lincoln had rented a pew, was the candidate of the moderates who sought to heal the breach.[53]

On the first ballot, and by a sizeable majority, Stanton was elected Moderator. The Assembly proceeded to deny seats to Robinson, Wilson, and others who had signed the *Declaration and Testimony*. . . . Gurley, moving from moderation to apply a *coup de grace*, spearheaded an effort to have the Assembly dissolve any lower court that kept a signer of the document among its members.[54]

Louisville Presbytery, in defiance, voted to renounce the authority of the General Assembly. The Synod of Kentucky, meeting in Henderson in October, found itself locked out of the church building when the *Declaration and Testimony* . . . signers were not seated. It met at the Cumberland Presbyterian Church nearby and at the Methodist Church in order to adjourn to a place of seeming safety—Second Presbyterian, Lexington.[55]

In November at Second in Lexington, the Synod tried again to meet. Evidently Synod applied the tests General Assembly had legislated, for it noted certain elders were seated "declaring adhesion to the Synod and the General Assembly." But procedural warfare took place nonetheless. The Stated Clerk of Synod, S. S. McRoberts, refused the request of the moderator, R. S. Breck, to read "the names of all the constituent elements of the Synod" including those who had been barred from sitting on courts and those who had renounced the authority of the courts. Breck assumed the position of Stated Clerk himself, and R. J. Breckinridge protested. He and Ruling Elder George Wood were "cried down by a loud clamor in the house."[56] Breck asked W. W. Hill, of Anchorage, to read the roll. All the *Declaration and Testimony* . . . people answered, while Assembly loyalists did not. After a bit more parliamentary confusion, Breck adjourned the meeting. When the dissidents left, the loyalists remained, and again Kentucky Presbyterians found themselves divided.[57]

The split occurred with much vituperation and bitterness at Synod level, but its impact for most Presbyterians in Kentucky was felt in sessions and congregations.

The Cumberland Alternatives

During the antebellum years, the Cumberland Presbyterian Church made great strides in its missionary efforts. In 1830, Cumberland congregations had existed in six states—Kentucky and Tennessee, where the church began, together with Alabama, Illinois, Indiana, and Missouri. The movement resisted gathering statistics, as many sects and beginning denominations have done. Even so, historians of that communion estimate from good evidence that about 100,000 communicants in sixteen states, three territories, and two Indian nations in 1859 shared allegiance to the Cumberland Presbyterian Church. The Cumberlands had also begun a mission in Liberia by that time.[58]

Cumberland Presbyterians in Kentucky evangelized their neighbors and the denomination did grow. Especially in Logan Presbytery and in the area around Princeton the new churches arose. But Cumberland Kentuckians also moved west, and soon there were more Cumberland Presbyterian Church members in Illinois than in the commonwealth which fed its growth.[59]

Cumberland Presbyterians had begun a college in Princeton for training ministerial candidates and others in the liberal arts. The Reverend Franceway Ranna Cossitt, a major proponent of the school in 1825, also subscribed to the principle that all students should engage in manual labor while they studied. Chartered in 1826, the Cumberland College had engaged Cossitt to lead the enterprise and promised money to support it. Misunderstandings about money, and resistance to the uniform requirements of manual labor, plagued the early life of the school. After Cossitt left, a brief respite in the instition's history occurred when Richard Beard and the Reverend A. J. Baird made successive efforts to provide stability and solvency for it. But in 1858 the Cumberland Presbyterian Church severed ties with Cumberland College. The continuing controversy centering on leadership for this school provided an almost perpetual dilemma for the denomination until the time of the Civil War, and it soured the spirit of some Kentucky Cumberland Presbyterians in the process.[60]

The Civil War cost Cumberland Presbyterians dearly, as it cost Old School Presbyterians. With membership in Confederate states and Union states, with strong regional identification to border areas, the Cumberland Presbyterian Church was forced to confront issues of division and loss of support. The mission in Liberia floundered for lack of funds, and a new effort in the Middle East proved stillborn in the chaos.[61]

When the war came, however, the Cumberland Church chose to remain united. A moderate leader, the Reverend Milton Bird, guided the General Assembly during the years 1861–1865. He directed that the roll call of all presbyteries continue. That action, together with the subsequent appointment of ex-Confederates to positoins of responsibility in the church during Reconstruction times, enabled the Cumberland Presbyterian Church to move through the national cataclysm with relative equanimity.[62]

At the 1861 Assembly, the denomination "prayed for God's blessing through troublous times." At the 1862 Assembly, in Owensboro, delegates did not come from Confederate states, but a sizeable number of delegates did come from border states to temper the positions of those from Union areas. Moderator Bird traveled through portions of Tennessee to assure Southerners of the continued fellowship of the church. While memorials did pass declaring loyalty to the Union, because Northerners controlled Assemblies in 1864 and 1865, their provisions were not enforced when Southern Cumberland Presbyterians attended the Assembly of 1866. Ex-Confederates were not requested to make "repentance and humiliation before God," as the 1864 pronouncement had stipulated. Rather, as the court gathered again in

Owensboro, 67 of 150 delegates who came from formerly Confederate states, and about forty delegate from Kentucky and Missouri presbyteries, merely signed the roll and responded much as though it were just another Assembly.[63]

The Cumberland Presbyterian Church did not escape postwar recriminations altogether. But by arguing that civil government had settled the matters of slavery and the right to withdrawal from the Union (both decided in the negative) the church could move to other business. An 1869 narrative on the "State of Religion" declared that "sectional animosities" had been buried, and the "bonds of Christian fellowship" had been reestablished in the communion.[64]

The Cumberland Presbyterian Church, whose judicious leadership permitted a Presbyterian alternative to division during the war, took a more precipitous step afterward when it excised black Cumberland Presbyterians to make them form a separate "Colored Cumberland Presbyterian Church."

In Henderson in 1868, a convention of Cumberland Presbyterians who were black expressed interest in forming a separate denomination. Whether these sentiments represented a reaction to Assembly pronouncements of 1868, or whether black leaders took initiative, cannot be determined from evidence available. What remains clear is the fact that when subsequent conventions in Huntsville, Alabama, and Murfreesboro, Tennessee met, there resulted the formation of a separate Colored Cumberland Presbyterian Church. White church leaders assumed all blacks had to belong to that separate church. Again, statistics for that denomination do not indicate very accurately the situation, but about 3,000 communicants were numbered when the Colored Cumberland Presbyterian Church Assembly met in 1874. It evidently gained in strength to number about 15,000 by the turn of the century. Just how many black Presbyterians in Kentucky were members of the Colored Cumberland Presbyterian Church is uncertain. The white denomination in 1887 did contribute money to a school in Bowling Green for "Colored Cumberland Presbyterians," and a history written in 1888 still spoke in proprietary terms about "our colored ministers" meeting in that city.[65] Thus while they did not divide sectionally, the Cumberland Church did separate on the basis of race.

The Cumberland alternatives prevailed for that more congregationally-oriented wing of Kentucky Presbyterianism. And in a sense "border" religion proved a different experience for them. However, the mainstream of Kentucky Presbyterianism was engaged in acrimony after the Civil War, and that story remains a part of the "border" church.

Dr. Edward O. Guerrant (1838–1916), physician and minister who led home missions in Eastern Kentucky especially. His work resulted in the organization of scores of congregations, hospitals, and schools.

Typical Presbyterian choir, 1870. This choir served Second Presbyterian Church, Lexington, in the first years of such special organizations.

CHAPTER **6.**

Reconstruction Realignments

The Cumberland Presbyterian Church may have avoided schism by simply calling the roll, but the Old School Assembly had elected to exacerbate differences in loyalty. Thus the Reconstruction era, though it scarcely affected Kentucky in the manner of other ex-slave states, nonetheless meant a new configuration developed for what had been a strong Old School synod. Under the new alignments lay a number of acrimonious lawsuits and much hostility. The pain engendered cannot be mapped, but the course of the institutions can, both on congregational and synodwide levels.

The silver lining for the Southern Church, if it can be so termed, came in the provision of needs for deep South churches by their new colleagues in ministry from Kentucky. During the most severe period of Reconstruction, Kentucky Presbyterians sent tons of food staples and much clothing South. They gave of their money to help rebuild church buildings destroyed in Georgia, Mississippi, and South Carolina. In general, they gave leadership and a measure of hope to the more decimated segments of the PCUS.

Into the Southern Church

As signers of the *Declaration and Testimony* . . . were excluded, and excluded themselves, from the Synod Kentucky, they formed an

''Independent Synod'' in the state. VanderVelde counted 100 Ruling and Teaching Elders in the new organization at its inception. Only 60 of the members of the Synod remained affiliated with the Old School Church—32 ministers and 28 ruling elders. A number of the pastors who remained were professors at Danville Seminary or Centre; only seven were regular pastors of congregations. In brief, the new Independent Synod claimed the vast majority of congregational pastors. Of 11,250 communicants in the Synod of Kentucky at the time, only 1800 were members of congregations where pastors remained in the Old School, PCUSA.[1]

The Independent Synod saw itself standing ''in mediation between the Church of the North and of the South.''

> This Synod . . . expresses, on the one hand, its sympathy and its readiness to co-operate with such conservative brethren in the Northern Assembly as desire to return to the old paths; and on the other hand, its sympathy with, and readiness to assist to the utmost of its ability, the brethren of the Southern churches; and at the same time, expresses the hope that they will evince a readiness to co-operate with all Conservative men, North and South, in a common effort to restore the General Assembly as it was before the war, on the basis of those ancient conservative principles of Presbyterianism, for which this Synod is contending.[2]

The ''conservatism'' expressed by the Synod and its tentative existence were not met by equal sentiments from the Old School Assembly of 1867. Rather, that assembly effectively closed the door to a reunion by taking upon itself affirmation of the loyalists and by accusing dissidents of ''trifling with sacred interests.'' Old Schoolers also moved in rapid fashion toward union with the New School Assembly, accomplished in 1869.[3]

The Independent Synod of Kentucky met in Louisville following the Assembly, and a debate between Stuart Robinson and Samuel Wilson resulted in a decision to wait before uniting with any other body. But cordial correspondence began with the Southern Church. Some representatives attended the Southern Assembly of 1867, and they witnessed the union of the Presbytery of Patapsco (Maryland) with the body—the beginning of a move by the denomination to increase its territory beyond the original states of the late Confederacy.[4]

When Synod met in 1868, constituent presbyteries expressed differing degrees of enthusiasm for union. Each presbytery sent its own representative to the May 1869 meeting of the PCUS Assembly in Mobile. Thus effective decision-making occurred not in the independent Synod but rather in each presbytery. The Mobile Assembly did recognize and enroll the newcomers, and a momentous change took place very quietly.[5] In election of its Moderator the Assembly showed its opinion of the union—Stuart Robinson, who led the majority of Kentucky Presbyterians into the Southern Church, was elected. The Assembly likewise accepted the profferred invitation of Louisville's Second Presbyterian to host the following year's conclave. One researcher estimates that overall about 8,000 members in more than a hundred churches joined with the PCUS through these events.[6]

Some semblance of order reigned again in 1870 in Kentucky Presbyterianism. Most of the legal suits had been resolved. Most of the bitter fighting was over. Confusion still existed in the names of organizations. The Synod of Kentucky (PCUSA) had three presbyteries—Transylvania, Ebenezer, and West Lexington. The Synod of Kentucky (PCUS) possessed seven presbyteries—Transylvania, Ebenezer, West Lexington, Louisville, Paducah, Muhlenburg, and Central Ohio.[7]

The coming of the PCUS Assembly that year to Louisville represented a rather late chapter in border Presbyterianism. The congregation had just completed a new building, at Second and Broadway. During the meetings a trio of distinguished visitors arrived bearing news from the Northern Church: Dr. J. C. Backus of Baltimore, W. E. Dodge the industrialist, and Dr. Henry Van Dyke of New York. They bore a message from the PCUSA Assembly, meeting concurrently in Philadelphia. The PCUSA sought to open correspondence with a view to union, but the Southern Church responded negatively. Southerners concerned themselves primarily with their own missions and institutions, setting the pattern for decades to come.[8]

Walnut Church Case, etc.

The most notorious, and perhaps the most painful, of the congregational splits occurred in the Walnut Street Presbyterian Church in

Louisville. The fight was just one of the hundreds which took place, but following it in some detail elucidates the depth and the contentiousness of the border strife.

In the midst of the building program and with only the church basement fully completed, the congregation of Louisville's Walnut Street Presbyterian Church (also known as the Third Presbyterian Church) met for worship on 27 August 1854. While the Reverend Robert Morrison, their temporary supply, was preaching, a severe cyclone or tornado leveled the yet uncompleted structure above their heads and rained rubble on the assembly. Fifteen members of the congregation died in the holocaust, and another score of persons suffered severe injuries. Among the dead were Jane Martin, whose husband, John served as elder; Adaline Vilderbee and her three children; and a number of other men and women. The remainder of the congregation determined, however, to "consider this affliction a call of God to greater devotion, zeal and activity in the service of Christ."[9]

Help came from other Old School Presbyterian congregations, as well as from the community in general—money, offers of pastoral services, and new hands for replacing those lost in the storm. Notable among the new people who joined the congregation at this time was Elder B. F. Avery, who had been a Louisville plow manufacturer since 1847. Formerly of Second Presbyterian Church, Avery subsequently became a principal in the church split of 1866. After a year during which Dr. M. R. Miller supplied the church, the Reverend John H. Rice was called and installed as pastor. He undertook work in the still decimated church on 3 May 1856. Until he resigned, Rice assisted the congregation in achieving at least temporary self-sufficiency and a modicum of calm.[10]

The Civil War elicited much Southern sympathy among the members of the Walnut Street Church, as among Kentucky Presbyterians in general. However, B. F. Avery and many of the other church members remained Unionists, albeit, reluctant ones. They sided with the loyalist party of Kentuckians. As the American War of Secession "progressed," internal friction increased within the Walnut Church due to the pro-Confederate stance of the Stated Supply, the Reverend William T. McElroy. Engaged by the session from 1862 for a succession of six month contracts, McElroy did refrain from preaching his allegiance from the pulpit until a salary dispute arose in 1865. Also during the time of the war, Mrs. Susan Furgison was received as a member "having arrived from Paris, her former residence." Mrs. Furgison, according to Session Minutes, was a black "free" woman; this notation of her color and "status" evidences some discussion, if not disagreement, on the matter of her admission.[11] Session members remaining from the time of McElroy's appointment through the occasion of the initial split, (August 1861, until March 1865), were T. J. Hackney, carpenter Joseph Gault (Galt), lumber dealer John Martin, and John Watson.[12] In addition, the Minutes show that Avery was the church treasurer on 28 September 1864 and presumably had been serving in that capacity for some years.[13]

Efforts of the pro-Southern session majority in March 1865, to call McElroy as the permanent pastor of the church, met with stiff resistance from members of the congregation.[14] These elders, Martin, Gault, and Watson met with McElroy in the absence of Hackney and unanimously recommended McElroy to the congregation. When a majority of the congregation declined to issue the call, Watson, Martin, and Gault again met with McElroy and instituted a special 4:00 P.M. meeting on the following Sunday to replace evening service. Furthermore, they elected a pro-Southerner and business partner of Gault, George Fulton, to replace Avery as church treasurer. Avery, and perhaps D. McNaughton, another pro-Union man, received formal accusations from the session of "conduct being unchristian in Spirit, and injurious in its tendencies." Avery, McNaughton, and by August 23, Hackney, in addition, signed a petition for the removal of McElroy as Stated Supply. The session majority retaliated by charging Avery formally with "Schism, Insubordination, Contumacy, and Deception." They likewise charged their outvoted colleague Hackney with "Making False Statements," "Criminal Duplicity of Conduct," and "Schismatic Conduct." They drew up exhaustive lists of specifics to accompany each charge. The words of the charges and specifications were vague, yet discernible in intent: "He has endeavored to arouse opposition to the action of the Session by appealing to political prejudices, and by attributing political and other improper motives to the members thereof."[15]

Poor John Martin (whose wife had earlier died in the act of worship) now found himself caught in the midst of a human-fashioned cyclone of comparable proportions. He evidently did attend the subsequent "hearings," but then his name drops from the Minutes and the story. Whether he died or simply lost the will to contend cannot be determined from the records at hand.

As for the "hearings," they consumed at least six lengthy meetings of the Walnut Street Session. Witnesses testified that Avery had indeed resisted in supporting session recommendations to call McElroy. In fact, he had even invited one member, Mr. Browning, to "go to the 2nd ch. and hear Mr. Young."[16] The fact that Avery had formerly attended Second Church and served as an elder there was not articulated in the hearing.

In addition to this very personal questioning of Avery, the "hearing" inquired into Avery's statements regarding McElroy. Allegedly he had told members of the congregation that McElroy changed from being a loyal Unionist to becoming a pro-Southerner.[17]

The hearing promised to last forever, and the list of prospective witnesses grew, but according to indications in the Minutes, Avery himself soon stopped attending them. The need for such meetings was precluded, however, when a commission of the Synod of Kentucky was appointed to investigate charges and countercharges in the congregation.[18]

According to the court summary, the Synod Committee possessed powers "to call a congregational meeting for the purpose of electing additional ruling elders, calling a pastor, or choosing a stated supply. . . . "[19] Gault, Watson, and McElroy met on New Year's Eve 1865, and resolved as a session that they "do hereby prohibit said meeting as unlawful, unconstitutional, unjust, and revolutionary." They appointed Gault to "have the house closed against said meeting."[20] The committee of Synod, with a majority of the congregation, met on the sidewalk in front of the locked building. Thus on 2 January 1866, Walnut Street Presbyterian Church elected J. A. Leach, B. F. Avery, and D. McNaughton as new session members. The pro-Northerners ordained and installed them the following Sunday with the help of the Reverends J. L. McKee and J. C. Young, representatives of the Synod.[21]

Immediately the validity of the ordinations and the installations was denied by Watson, Gault, McElroy, the moderator, and by George Fulton and Henry Farley (who with Avery had been previously the trustees of the congregation's property). Further, the four pro-Southerners, with moderator McElroy making five, brought a series of formal charges against the Synod representatives, McKee and Young.[22]

Meanwhile Avery, et. al., filed a bill at Louisville Chancery Court against their exclusion as session members. Three and one half months later, on 15 June 1866, the Chancellor opined that Avery, Leach, and McNaughton be recognized as elders and included in all decision making. Watson and his colleagues at the same time attended the newly organized Presbytery of Louisville and there received permission for McElroy to continue as pastor. They likewise received confirmation that their own possession of the church building was valid. Therefore they continued to exclude the Averyites from worship and meetings. Avery complained again to the magistrate, who ordered a court marshal to take possession of the building. This he did on July 23, and he sought to make provisions for both parties to meet in the church separately. But Avery, Leach, and McNaughton sought as a session majority to exclude the Watsonites, and met with success in their attempt. The Watsonites, with the Walnut Street Church Minute book in hand, met at the church again on August 23, September 30, and November 12. However, by the time of their January meeting, the pro-Southerners had moved to meet in the chapel of Louisville's Male High School.[23]

By now Watson had appealed the Chancery decision, and the Kentucky Court of appeals reversed the opinion. The case was "remanded for proper corrective proceedings . . . and final judgment." On 28 February 1868, the Avery adherents charged in Chancery that Gault, Watson, Fulton, etc. "had voluntarily withdrawn" from the church. A month later the chancellor awarded the property to the pro-Unionists. Again appealed, the Kentucky Appeals Court ordered the chancellor to approve use of the property by the Watson, Gault faction exclusively. Chancery court, under the higher authority, decided to restore the property " . . . to Farley, Fulton, and Avery, or a majority of them, as trustees, and to Watson, Galt [sic] , and Hackney, or a majority of them, as ruling elders." This ruling, rendered on 18 September 1868, effectively ended the first lawsuit.[24]

On 17 July 1868, a suit was filed against Watson and his party sympathetic to the *Declaration and Testimony* . . . but also against Avery and the Walnut members loyal to the Old School. The three plaintiffs were William Jones and his wife Catherine, and her sister, Miss Eleanor Lee. Lee, formerly a resident of Kentucky, had published at least one book of poetry with Catherine.[25] Now all three had moved to Indiana, across the Ohio River from the Kentucky church, and though members of the congregation, as out-of-state members they could file a Federal suit. From the record it certainly appears that Avery, McDougall, McPherson, and Ashcraft were defendants friendly to the plaintiffs, for they cooperated in every way.

Watson, Gault, and their group should be restrained, argued the suit, from interfering in the regular activities of the church. Hackney, Avery, and the other pro-Northerners admitted in response they had failed in their duty to keep disrupters from interfering. They had assumed the matter would be handled in the courts. The ''real'' defendants— Watson, Gault, Fulton, and Farley—denied every allegation and argued further that the Jones couple and Lee moved to Indiana merely to file the suit.

Federal District Court decided in favor of the plaintiffs. Watson, Gault, and their newly elected colleagues (including Joseph Given), were not to be privileged officers of the church, nor was the man they asked to lead them in worship, Dr. Yandell, duly installed as pastor. Thus in every respect affiliates of the pro-Southern presbytery and the newly emerging synod did not have rights either to the property or to the determination of staff or program.

Louisville's T. W. Bullitt, a lawyer of considerable local renown, argued in his appeal of the decision that Watson and the others he represented would receive justice only when this new suit was found spurious. The Circuit Court had no jurisdiction because the matter, an intrastate dispute, had been settled in an appropriate court. He argued also that ecclesiastical courts are ''voluntary associations,'' and that the minority adhered to representative government which reflected true Presbyterianism.

For Jones and the Avery party, B. H. Bristow and John Marshall Harlan, later himself a justice of the Supreme Court, argued that it was the majority who adhered to the Presbytery, Synod, and General Assembly true to the original intent of establishing the trusteeship. Thus secular courts have no right to intervene.[26]

With the Chief Justice not sitting on the case, and with two justices dissenting, the court affirmed the rights of the Jones, Avery, pro-Northern group, to hold the property and to govern the church.[27]

The doctrine of "implied trust," the principle that a lower court in a connectional denomination held title to property in behalf of the highest judicatory, was the result of this particular case.[28] But other churches and institutions divided in Kentucky, some fighting for possession of property and others parting in relative equanimity.

In Paris, for example, where a comparatively strong New School congregation had reunited in 1859 with its Old School competitor, the division in 1868–69 was made easier by the existence of two Presbyterian church structures. Soon the anti-Assembly congregation built another edifice.[29] In Louisville's stronger congregations, a great majority at First, two-thirds at Second, and most of Fourth Presbyterian denounced their connection to the Assembly.[30] In Lexington, both First and Second split initially, but then First gravitated toward the Southern denomination while Second remained in the Old School Assembly.[31] Almost every conceivable type of division, split, and settlement took place somewhere in the state.

Centre College and Danville Seminary

The Walnut Street Church case had its major educational parallel in the institutional litigation over control of Centre College and the Danville Seminary which had been formed to accompany it. During and immediately after the Civil War, enrollment at the schools had shrunk considerably. But both the PCUSA minority in Kentucky Presbyterianism and the majority that came in time to join with the PCUS sought to claim the college and the seminary.

Centre College had changed during the 1820s from a state-supported institution to a private Presbyterian institution. Under the leadership of James McChord and Samuel Finley, Centre simply had not attracted the numbers of students and faculty, or the financial support, necessary to become a viable context for higher education.[32] So the third president of Centre, Jeremiah Chamberlain, in 1824 had overseen an agreement between the General Assembly of the state and the Synod of Kentucky (PCUSA) which enabled the church court to assume complete responsibility for the school in 1830.[33] Once the Presbyterians took structural control of it, they took pains not only to elect responsible trustees, but also to hear extended reports at each Synod meeting on the activities of faculty and the curriculum of instruction.[34] Synod even received information enumerating and naming books acquired for Centre's library. Throughout antebellum days, however, the state continued to help fund an attendant School for the Deaf which remained in Danville under the purview of the trustees of Centre College.[35]

As Centre became strictly Presbyterian, it maintained excellence in instruction while it expanded. Presbyterians and many others who simply wanted quality education in Kentucky, supported the work of the college. They sent their sons to be students, and they gave funds to undergird the enterprise.[36]

Centre also gained in health and reputation under the administration of John C. Young, who became its President in 1830 and remained in that office until his death in 1857. In the words of W. C. P. Breckinridge, the son of Robert Breckinridge and a graduate of Centre, Young was the "dominant, controlling, moulding spirit in the college" for that time. Young, born and reared in Pennsylvania, came to Kentucky at the recommendation of John C. Breckinridge to become pastor of the McChord Presbyterian Church. Young, then, lived practically next door when he received the call to lead the school. In 1834 the Presbyterian Church in Danville also called John C. Young to become its pastor. Therefore for pre-ministerial students he modeled what it meant to be a minister while he superintended their instruction. For other students he made certain that education occurred in behalf of their vocations.[37]

When the Old School/New School split occurred, Young and the other leaders in the school and church remained staunchly with thc Old School assembly. Centre became increasingly a bastion of Old School thought. When Young became moderator of that Assembly, he and Robert J. Breckinridge collaborated to have Danville chosen as the place in which to locate "a Theological Seminary of the first class." Breckinridge was chosen for one professorship, as already indicated. E. P. Humphrey, who had been instrumental in the early life of Louisville's Second Presbyterian Church, was called to teach "Biblical and Ecclesiastical History." Too, after a few false starts, the school enlisted the Reverend Joseph G. Reasor to teach "Oriental and Biblical Literature." Stuart Robinson served on the faculty two years, and Stephen Yerkes joined in 1857.[38]

Centre College and Danville Seminary experienced a few years of remarkable achievement before the Civil War interrupted continuity and decimated the student body. The seminary quickly attracted excellent students, as the college had already. In addition, the founding of the Henderson Female Institute the following year in Danville did not hurt the recruitment of either men or women. But both the college and the seminary, not to mention the Henderson Institute, attracted many students from the South.[39]

When Breckinridge so embodied Unionist loyalties, and when court cases resolved the contest for control in favor of the PCUSA (Northern), Southerners and Kentuckians moving into the PCUS naturally avoided the institutions. The Southerners initiated a new, rival university and they planned to open a competitive seminary at a later date.[40]

Centre and Danville Seminary limped along. In 1869 Centre graduated only four men; in 1870, only seven; in 1871, nine.[41] Class size at Centre College improved a bit in the later years of the decade, as the steady hand of Dr. Ormond Beatty held the course of it. Beatty, who had himself graduated from Centre, had taught mathematics, chemistry, and natural philosophy.[42]

At the Danville Seminary, hard times proved even harder. In 1868 and 1869, summer courses were the only occasions of formal instruction; in 1870 when a full faculty of three arrived under the direction of Stephen Yerkes, only six students attended. Again in 1871–1874 the school maintained a skeleton enrollment, an institutional casualty of the border friction which retained some force among Presbyterians.[43]

Both Centre and Danville had depended largely upon Northern faculty and Southern students when attracting persons from outside Kentucky. Border strife inhibited the mix, but as the nature of the denominations changed again, the institutions gathered momentum once more.

PART III.
Heartland

Mrs. Mary D. Irvine (1865–1935), a lifetime member of the Danville First Presbyterian Church, pioneered in founding women's organizations among Southern Presbyterians.

Miss Lucy McGowan (1863–1954), a leader throughout the state in missions activities and one of the early members of Crescent Hill Presbyterian, Louisville.

CHAPTER 7.

Into Heartland Presbyterianism

It is a pleasant irony that Presbyterians in Kentucky almost ceased their internecine struggles during the very years that have been aptly labeled the state's "Decades of Discord: 1865–1900."[1] The denominations entered what might be termed "heartland Protestantism" during those very years. The term "heartland" carries appropriate connotations in several respects when used to describe this third period of Kentucky Presbyterianism. Literally, piety and geography became increasingly central. Orthodoxy became less of an issue. Kentucky also became a central and important locus for agitation and action in behalf of Presbyterian union. The very place that focused church splits began in the latter years of the nineteenth century to foster the healing of splits.

After the establishment of the two almost co-extensive Synods of Kentucky in 1866, 1867, no further schisms of major proportions have occurred for the Presbyterians. A number of reasons for such a change can be proffered. The Presbyterians could simply have worn themselves out in fighting before, during, and immediately after the Civil War. Alternatively, they could have become stable because they had also become thoroughly acculturated in American life. But the explanation most suitable to the facts argues that Presbyterians began to engage in "church program" during Reconstruction. They experimented with a new and distinctive style of evangelism which changed their perspective. Absorbed in program and mission efforts, they left church family arguments largely to others.

Church Programs

Throughout their history, Presbyterians have formed committees and organized societies within churches for various purposes. But in the 1870s committees, societies, and programs took on an ever-increasing level of importance for the congregation.

As just one of the churches' structures, the Sunday school represented this change. In the 1820s and afterward Sabbath schools had existed. In the 1870s and afterwards, they became the center of much more activity and congregational life. On a national scale, the resurrection of Sunday schools began with the work of Dwight L. Moody and his "Illinois Band" in the late 1860s.[2]

In 1872, the Uniform—or International—Lesson system began to infuse Kentucky Sunday schools with a Bible-centered, but also a catholic curriculum. Many of the Southern congregations resisted these ecumenically-designed lessons at first even though Presbyterian presses published them. The congregations complained that they did not stress sufficiently the Bible itself, or they did not allow for enough catechetical instruction.[3]

Even very small congregations possessed Sunday schools and they faithfully reported to Synod each year the number of teachers and "scholars" involved. In the U.S. Synod, where most of the membership existed, an 1881 report indicated 731 teachers and 5,542 scholars enrolled. The Committee on Sunday schools for the Synod was still urging use of denominational material as curriculum that year—the Westminster Catechisms and Confession of Faith, as well as the *Earnest Worker* and the *Children's Friend*.[4]

Larger congregations developed sophisticated programs for various age groups. Usually a member of the session served as "superintendent of the Sunday school," although it was not uncommon for a deacon or another male member to serve. Sometimes a woman headed the "Primary Department" or in other ways led the teaching of younger children. Some of the more affluent congregations paid a stipend to heads of the departments.[5]

Organization of the Sunday schools frequently followed the form advocated by the International Sunday School Association: Beginner (pre-school), Primary (grades 1–3), Junior (grades 4–6), Intermediate (grades 7–9), and Senior (grades 9–12). Adult classes were commonly segregated according to age and sex. In 1910, for example, Crescent Hill Presbyterian Church in Louisville had a "Woman's Bible Class" under the direction of Mrs. W. E. Blackburn. The score or so members met for Sunday school, but they also met each Thursday morning for further study. That congregation also had a "Men's Bible Class," which may have met during the week as well.[6]

A rare and fascinating glimpse into the nature of the adult classes across the state is afforded by the volumes collected from one teacher's lessons. The Men's Bible Class at Second Church in Louisville was taught for more than a decade by Helm Bruce, a lawyer and session member. A stenographer copied the words of the teacher, who spoke without notes and recited much of the Scripture from heart. The session then published his lessons sequentially, and copies were used by other teachers in the Southern church.[7]

"The purpose of this class," Bruce said, "is to read the Bible and try to understand it as a whole." He proceeded to interpret books and passages within them in terms of Presbyterian doctrine and "horse sense." He wanted to highlight "rules of conduct to live by" and considered that both Old and New Testaments gave many. Proverbs were mixed with the sayings of Jesus and with personal experiences, thematic and topical.[8]

By the 1910s the program orientation of Sunday schools extended into annual productions of Christmas pageants in some churches and periodic banquets in others. Routinely Sunday schools would gather for a beginning "assembly," led by the superintendent, and then split into various graded classes. A number of sanctuaries were modified to serve also as assembly halls.[9]

Kentucky Presbyterian John Stites presided when the Twelfth International Sunday School Convention took place in Louisville in 1908. He was elected by delegates from almost every state in the Union, as well as from all parts of Canada. Those responsible for various departments and programs of the Sunday school all gave glowing accounts of the work being done, ringing challenges to do that which was still needed. Programs in temperance, missions, teacher education, literacy, home life, home visitation, and "religious development of the Negro" represented just a portion of the activity. Thus the program of the Sunday school system generated spin-off programs in all these areas.[10]

The Sunday schools also generated interest in and support for "Societies of Christian Endeavor," self-governing bodies of those "too big to attend" the Sunday school. Christian Endeavor was ecumenical in a limited sense, with evangelical and Reformed, Disciples of Christ, and several other denominations sharing leadership with the Presbyterians. Begun in 1882, it soon had chapters in many Kentucky locales and enlisted a number of young people for leadership in the Presbyterian churches. Particular societies met in the churches, some at Sunday school time and others in the evenings. A number of congregations, including those in Ashland and Maysville, reported sponsoring "Junior Societies of Christian Endeavor" as well as "Senior Societies." The Ashland Societies were the sources of funds to "gasify" that church in 1900.[11]

Vacation Bible School, another part of the growing congregational program, began in a number of churches during the 1910s. Second Church in Louisville, with its considerable human and financial resources, opened perhaps the first Vacation Bible School in 1912. Mrs. James R. Skillman provided continual leadership for that program for forty years. It mixed Bible study and skills development in a six-week summer session. It also offered a large dose of recreation for the children, few of whom belonged in families of that congregation. Girls learned sewing; boys, woodworking; and all received time in the gymnasium and around the piano.[12]

Other churches quickly adopted Vacation Bible Schools as a vital part of their programs, though many kept their plans more modest. By 1920 a number of associations had arisen of community churches offering Vacation Bible School. The Louisville Association that year listed eleven churches—four of them Presbyterian. Doubtless most Vacation Bible School programs did not receive such specific attention; in fact, few seem to have been ever mentioned in session records.[13]

The proliferation of programs continued. All denominations conducted concerted fund drives early in the twentieth century, and synods and other institutions began capital programs, too. Sundays of special note included those for "Ministerial Relief" and "Sabbath Observance." "Every Member Canvass" campaigns were advocated about 1910 by synod committees on "Systematic Benevolence."[14]

Choirs, too, became a regular feature in Kentucky Presbyterian churches. Frequently special music began with installation of an organ and the collecting of a quartet. Affluent congregations sometimes paid all four members, and a few even hired double quartets. Volunteer choirs characterized most smaller churches, and some larger ones resisted on principle the payment of "voices."[15]

Naturally the increasing complexity in program brought congregational needs for more trained personnel. Directors of Christian (or Religious) Education became a common part of the staffs of even rural churches, with several frequently sharing one person's services. Organists and choir directors became increasingly important as members of the professional staff. Too, the ability of the pastor to administer a church program became a prerequisite for many churches to function.[16]

Circles, Presbyterials, Synodicals

As previously indicated, women outnumbered men on church rolls throughout Kentucky history. But only in "heartland" structure did they begin to exert any formal leadership on a local or connectional level. Cumberland Presbyterians even ordained a woman as a minister, but more commonly women exercised limited leadership through their own organizations. Their quasi-independent organizations were based upon the older informal pattern of a few neighbors gathering to talk or work on a project together. These "circles," primary identification units, were gathered into "unions" at a congregational level to focus on missions at home and abroad. The USA churches, though fewer, offered the earlier opportunities for organization of what was then called "woman's work." Later the PCUS and CPC churches followed suit, but Kentucky women stood out as pioneers in that enterprise.

Long before the Civil War, women had gathered in groups to learn about the Bible, mission work, and needs of the church. American Bible Society chapters had been open to women since the 1810s and "Female Benevolent Societies," had been advocated by the 1815 Assembly.[17] But not until 1875 was there a synodical organization in Kentucky, sanctioned by the Synod of Kentucky (PCUSA) and an auxiliary to the Women's Board of Foreign Missions of New York. Mrs. S. J. Look served as an early president of the Kentucky Synodical. In its first annual report, published in 1877, the Women's Missionary Society of Kentucky had channeled $1800 into foreign and domestic mission enterprise.[18]

When the Home Mission Synodical Society was formed in 1885, it consisted of Presbyterials in all areas of the state.[19] The Louisville Presbyterial, evidently the oldest from its 1879 organization, also proved the most active at the time. Subsequently, Ebenezer Presbyterial had coalesced in 1881 around interest in Pikeville College and other opportunities for giving. The Transylvania Presbyterial was contributing to the Women's Executive Committee in 1882 but its records go back only to 1887.[20]

In the Southern Church, the women in the Augusta congregation gathered their sisters from Ebenezer Presbytery's churches in 1894. Mrs. Bell R. Cleveland led the effort, and she obtained permission from the members of presbytery for its inception. The Ebenezer Union, according to one historian, discovered that "those from whom opposition was expected were the staunch supporters from the beginning."[21]

With help from various pastors, including Dr. Green of Danville, Women of Louisville Presbytery organized a union in 1899. Names of a number of pioneers in the work were recorded by Mary Irvine of Danville, who should have known well their contribution: Mrs. Charlton Rogers, Mrs. R. C. Davis, Mrs. Mary H. Tarry, Miss Louise Speed, Miss Lucy McGowan, and Miss Mary Blain. Irvine paid special tribute to the work of Eleanor T. Little, who sought to interest women in the establishment of a Juvenile Court, playgrounds accessible to the poor, a good public school system, and missions to other places.[22]

A Presbyterial in West Lexington Presbytery followed meetings of the Missionary Society for the First Presbyterian Church, Lexington, which began in 1890. Evidently it took fifteen years to overcome some resistance from men in that court, for a full-fledged organization did not begin until 1905. The Presbyterial of Transylvania Presbytery was finally initiated in 1907, after threatened opposition forced its postponement from 1900. Paducah Presbyterial started the same year, and Muhlenburg, 1908, completed the necessary organizations from which to form a Synodical in 1911.[23]

One of the effective leaders in the movement to enable an organization of women in the PCUS was Mary Irvine herself. From Spencer

County, she had received formal education at the Shelbyville Female Academy. From her Danville home, she functioned through the years as both an agitator for "women's work" as a formal part of the congregation's life and as a clearing house for information about the efforts of women elsewhere.

Mary Irvine was elected to chair the forming committee for a Synodical, then to represent the body in denominational gatherings. Lucy McGowan, the first President of the Kentucky Synodical, served on the Woman's Advisory Committee of the PCUS, as did Alice Eastwood, who became Secretary for the body.[24]

The circles, presbyterials, and synodicals did offer women a chance to become formal leaders in their own rights. Perspectives from the 1890s may illumine the "auxiliary" side of the enterprise, but in formation and sustenance the Women of the Church became (perhaps still remain) the primary source of training female leaders for the denominations.[25]

It is easy to forget that the circles, presbyterials and synodicals existed for home and foreign missions first, not just to train women in leadership. When Lucy McGowan was asked to become the Synodical Woman Visitor, her job was to organize all kinds of societies for the churches—Sunday schools, mission-interest groups, and circles. The heartland church emphasized mission and worked diligently in evangelism.[26]

The Southern Synodical, on its own and in cooperation with other states' organizations, in the 1920s began to sponsor programs itself. The Synodical President initiated the making of an annual report to the Synod also, beginning in 1921. Emma D. Cockerham, the first woman to address the PCUS Synod, told with pride of the youth conference held in Danville that summer, evidently the first of its kind in the state.[27] In 1923, an even more ambitious convocation gathered black women from across the state at Lincoln Institute. White Cross service began that year also, and the Synodical reported 21,142 members in 93 auxiliaries at that time. Their statistics included a full score of programmatic items, "Auxiliaries Observing Day of Prayer for Missions," for example, and "Church Prayer Calendar Used."[28]

The movement in the heartland church toward program had a purpose though. Just as the work of both Synodicals alerted women to mission needs, so the whole church spent a considerable portion of its energy on various programmatic missionary endeavors.[29] By the same token, women contributed immensely to the new institutions which the heartland church developed and maintained.

Central University and Louisville Seminary

When control of Centre College and Danville Seminary remained with the PCUSA, those who had joined with the PCUS smarted under the decision. Sympathetic voices claimed that Southern Presbyterians merely wanted to "erect an educational institution to take the place of that which they regarded as unjustly taken from them."[29] In fact, the Southern Presbyterian leaders, including Stuart Robinson, Bennett Young, and Judge H. W. Helm, probably desired to begin an institution that would outshine Centre and Danville. They met in April, 1871, concurrently with the assembly of the PCUS Synod and organized to raise funds for the new school. They resisted attempts to have the college subject to Synod authority, save in the faculty of ethics and morals which they hoped would develop into a seminary to rival Danville. The charter granted, the Boards of Curators and Trustees elected the Rev. Robert L. Breck of Richmond as Chancellor and the Rev. J. W. Pratt, who had served previously at the University of Alabama as a professor of English and as President; they selected Richmond as the site of the new college.[30]

Working hastily, Breck and Pratt managed to open the Central University in the fall of 1874. Ambitious plans for the university envisioned a College of Arts and Letters, a College of Law with a Preparatory Department, and a College of Medicine to be located in Louisville. The university built a modest library collection, a museum collection of moderate value, and several buildings as offices and classrooms. The Law College remained miniscule in proportion, seldom numbering a dozen students. The College of Medicine fared better. Able to attract competent faculty and students it opened an attendant College of Dentistry in 1886.[31]

The university also envisioned the creation of a number of Presbyterian "high schools" to feed the various colleges. The initial charter provided for six, and the Preparatory Department in Richmond was one of these. A second, the Jackson Collegiate Institute, began in 1890 in that Breathitt County town. When Mrs. S. P. Lees of New York City gave a substantial amount of money to the school, it was named in her honor.[32] A third school in Elizabethtown (1892) and a fourth in Middlesboro (1896) carried the plan further, although the Central University system never really achieved the goals set by ambitious founders.[33]

A bit more than nostalgia for the Confederacy motivated the organization of the schools and kept them going. Kentucky needed more institutions of learning, and both the state and nation needed good leadership in all areas. The memory of the ''Gray'' did not hurt, however; and in an era of national expansionism most Presbyterians did not question the militancy of the USA. All the preparatory schools taught ''Military Science'' and cooperated with the Federal Government who supplied guns and belts for the cadets. As late as 1900 the Central University Cadet Corps attended the annual Confederate Reunion, in Louisville that year. They drilled from the depot on Seventh Street down Broadway to the Presbyterian Seminary at the intersection of First. Old stalwart Bennett Young presented each of the officers of the student corps with ''the gray uniform, procured for the occasion.'' The account lamented that rain precluded the ''sham-battle and street parade'' that had been scheduled.[34]

The system of schools began with a flurry of activity, but support for them remained rather sporadic. Leadership by Pratt and Breck gave way to that of the Rev. L. H. Blanton. Blanton, who had been pastor in the Paris Church for a number of years, was called in 1880 to become Chancellor of the University.[35] He spent considerable energy helping to increase the endowment funds and moving responsibility for the schools' maintenance to the Synod of Kentucky (PCUS). In 1883, that Synod elected a Board of Curators to replace the two boards previously self-perpetuating within the ''Alumni Association.''

The Synod control also enabled the opening of the College of Theology in 1893 as another part of the University. As the Colleges of Medicine and Dentistry were progressing, the ''College of Theology'' was opened in Louisville. Its control was shared with the Synod of Missouri (PCUS), whose history in border struggles resembled that of Kentucky. The Louisville Presbyterian Theological Seminary began its first semester with 31 students and six faculty, an almost full-grown institution from the first.[36]

Thus the Central University came more to resemble Centre College in its structure. When the Panic of 1893 forced significant supporters of Central to renege on their financial commitments, and when enrollment at Central fell over a period of years, the Southern Church Synod and the PCUSA Synod agreed to consolidate resources.[37] Central University and the Louisville Presbyterian Seminary already fed the Presbyterian Church, though, even in their infancy. The training of leaders for the Presbyterians remained important, even when long terms of service in established pulpits became common. Missionaries were needed, as were new pastors in colonized churches.

Long Pastorates

Another characteristic of the heartland form of Presbyterianism was the long duration of pastorates. The stable nature of ministry doubtless reinforced congregational stability. Perhaps because particular churches changed little, their tendency was to hold on to a pastor. Perhaps also the shifts in ministry stand out less than in times of strife. Whatever the reason, congregation after congregation in Kentucky recorded long tenures for pastors during the last decades of the nineteenth century and the first of the twentieth.

In all synods (PCUS, PCUSA and CPC), some men remained twenty-five years in the same church; pastorates of fifteen and twenty years were not uncommon at all. Of course, there were exceptions. The Chestnut Street Church in Louisville, which changed its name in 1876 to the Broadway Tabernacle Presbyterian Church and in 1881 to the Warren Memorial Church, changed ministers even more frequently than title—calling five in about twenty years.[38] On the other hand, soon after the Old School/New School split, Sydney McRoberts moved to Stanford, Kentucky, and remained there for forty-eight years as pastor.[39] He remained there through much of the "border" era also.

At least three ministers deserve special attention in this connection. In the USA Synod, the Rev. William C. Condit remained at the First Presbyterian Church, Ashland, for fifty-five years as pastor and five more as Pastor Emeritus. The Rev. Edward M. Green served the First Presbyterian Church of Danville for forty-five, and another five as emeritus. And John N. Ervin served as pastor of the Dayton, Kentucky,

Presbyterian Church from 1879 until his death in 1944, a total of sixty-five years.

Condit, born in Washington, Kentucky, had graduated from Centre College and Princeton Seminary when he accepted the call at Ashland. His father had been minister of the Bethesda Church, predecessor to First, during the 1830s. W. C. Condit was one of only three pastors in Ebenezer Presbytery to remain in the PCUSA denomination when the split occurred. He then became the mission pastor for many little churches in the area, while at the same time he oversaw the growth of the Ashland Church from 60 members to 600 (1866–1916 figures). The local historian declared that "no movement for the progress or betterment of [Ashland's] people but sought and received his support." People in Ashland also remembered him as a peacemaker. "Where churches had trouble he was sent to hold meetings and adjust differences."[40]

Danville's Edward Green also became known as the "community pastor." From South Carolina originally, he had come to Danville via Columbia Seminary and a Confederate chaplaincy. He was able to share in the building of a chapel and areas for Sunday school classes. He also remained long enough for stories to arise around him of his wit and wisdom. When one member "fell to having visions" and asked, "Suppose the Lord tells me to go into your pulpit and preach some Sunday?" Green replied, according to the account, "You do whatever the Lord commands, but, remember, whenever you try to go into my pulpit, He is going to tell *me* to have you locked up."[41]

John N. Ervin of Dayton came from Ohio with formal education at Wooster College and Lane Seminary. According to newspapers, he became the first regular pastor of the struggling congregation at Dayton. He initiated a tradition of preaching "open air" services each summer; gradually that church grew from 30 to about 400 members. His service of sixty-five years in the same congregation was claimed by denominational officials to be a record in American Presbyterianism.[42]

Many others served for lengthy periods of time in places which enabled them to grow and to "be themselves" also. Such pastors, as community leaders, doubtless became generally broader in their spirit as time elapsed. But other characteristics marked the heartland church as well, including the acceptance of ecumenical revivalism.

Revivals and Colonies

Throughout the nineteenth century, Presbyterians in Kentucky had cooperated in revivals or held them on their own. During the last part of the nineteenth century, however, the use of revivals and special services became particularly pronounced. Perhaps the outstanding event in this respect occurred when Dwight L. Moody came to Louisville in January, 1888. It was, for him, a "smaller city" in the succession of crusades. But it gave impetus to a number of the city's congregations and encouraged other revivalists in their work.[43]

Moody, with Ira Sankey, the song leader, and an entourage of helpers, sponsored the building of a large wooden "tabernacle" beside the Warren Memorial Church. He gathered ministers from a number of denominations to sit with him on the platform and to counsel those convicted and converted in the meetings. A choir, collecting volunteers from downtown churches, helped promote the singing of "songs of Zion." Almost all the meetings were packed, with thousands turned away.[44]

The *Christian Observer*, informal organ of the Southern Church, lauded the fact that afternoon services took place in the Warren Memorial edifice itself. "It is well worth while for our friends in the country to come and catch some of this fire from above," the editors, F. B. and Thomas Converse concluded.[45] First, Second, Highland, Warren Memorial, and probably other Presbyterian congregations reported numbers of new members following the four-week long crusade.[46]

Moody, the master of revivalism in the English-speaking world, never received ordination. When Presbyterian churches followed up his crusade, however, they used ministers to preach in their sanctuaries. Dr. H. M. Scudder, pastor of the Carlisle, Kentucky, congregation, led a preaching "season" at First in Louisville.[47] The Rev. George Trenholm from Nashville kept the "fire from above" kindled at Second.[48] Angus McDonald from Henderson Presbyterian led protracted meetings at Third Presbyterian.[49] Portland Presbyterian joined Portland Methodist for continued preaching nightly. Parkland and Central both kept further meetings going for two weeks, and College Street leaders went calling on prospective members.[50] Walnut, Fourth, Highland and Jeffersontown Presbyterian churches all reported additions related to the Moody visit.

Altogether more than 800 were added to the rolls of Louisville churches during that winter.[51]

Big numbers and intense excitement surrounding Moody should not obscure the fact that congregations regularly relied on revivals for the refreshment of members and the conversion of the "almost persuaded." W. T. Spears of the Mayslick Church frequently preached in special meetings, and the *Observer* noted particularly "his success" at the Sharon Church in 1887.[52] Records from First Presbyterian in Lexington noted that George Pentecost in 1906 and Ernest Thacker in 1915 preached special services there.[53] Thacker, who had previously served the Stuart Robinson Church in Louisville, by 1915 was employed by the General Assembly of the PCUS to lead revivals across the denomination.[54]

But big numbers and intense excitement were expected at Second Presbyterian in Lexington when that church sponsored revivals by B. Fay Mills and Gipsy Smith. Mills had an Old School background, and he became one of the most efficient planners among the urban revivalists. He likewise preached corporate responsibility as well as individual repentance. The meetings were elsewhere in Lexington, but Second recorded 48 additions on account of them.[55]

The showman-singer, Gipsy Smith, did not come to Lexington until 1935, at the height of his fame (if not of his power). Those meetings were held in the sanctuary of Second, and Mrs. Fletcher Mann, "directress of the choir" at the time, assisted in planning and conducting the meetings.[56]

It was comparatively easy to attract large crowds in the cities of Kentucky and to enlist famous revivalists. More difficult was the revival work and church organization in rural areas.

Though it is difficult to assess the actual impact of these revivals on the life of the church, it is comparatively easy to see the difference between these "fires from above" and the revivals at the beginning of the century. Most apparent was the loss of any sacramental center for them, and the gain of new revivals more in and for the congregations. Where Cane Ridge, for example, focused on the eucharist at least in part, the Moody crusade kept any potentially divisive subject such as eucharist at arm's length.

Where Cane Ridge invited "whosoever will, come," Moody and

the ecumenical evangelicals, on the other hand, laid careful groundwork with invitations to congregations and sought to channel converts straight into local churches by having various sorts of ministers as counselors.[57]

The Presbyterian revivals represented an even stronger congregational focus, although still surprisingly little attention was paid to communion. Sessions regularly provided oversight of the evangelist, and local pastors received special attention from the outsider.

Despite differences, continuity with the earlier revivals remained to some degree. New persons and households different in background from those already confessing entered the Presbyterian fold. Naturally, such heterogeneity proved a blessing and a curse. In the frontier church, even the border church, resultant heterodox expressions received neutral if not hostile responses from Reformed leadership. In the heartland church, though, discipline seldom occurred, and a doctrinal latitude generally resulted. Acculturation? Christian charity? Emphasis on lifestyle over doctrine? Theological decadence? Whatever the appraisal of effects, these revivals helped to calm further an already gentler Christian community of faith. Revivals and the interests in conversion and church growth enabled Presbyterians to found many new congregations as they "colonized" in nearby communities and neighborhoods.

Heartland Presbyterians attached strong, positive connotations to the word "colonize." Strong congregations felt a responsibility to send groups of members to found Sunday schools, chapels, and churches. The nucleus of three congregations in Louisville came from Second Presbyterian in Louisville, for example—the Stuart Robinson Church, the Woodland Church, and the Westminster Church. Highland Presbyterian and Crescent Hill Presbyterian were also organized with substantial monetary and membership contributions from Second—all in the 1880s.[58]

Interesting, and typical of the colonizing efforts of local congregations, was the forming of a Second Presbyterian Church in Henderson. For a number of years, the leaders of First Church had conducted a Sunday school in the Chestnut Hill area of town. In 1884, twelve members of the First Church petitioned presbytery to form a separate congregation. During its first year, the new congregation built a house of worship and called a pastor. The salary of the pastor, $1,200, was paid by members of the new congregation, the First Presbyterian members through synod's committee, and the Ladies' Society of First. By June 1886, two hundred more members had been added to the roll of the Second Presbyterian Church. That congregation had begun to make contributions to missions and it had considered establishing an outpost Sunday school on its own.[59]

The two synods also employed ministers on a part-time basis to help begin new congregations in nearby communities. The Rev. S. D. Boggs was one, who served the Presbyterian Church in Catlettsburg in the 1880s. He was enlisted to begin a Sunday school and then a congregation in Hampton City, a town adjacent to his own. Members joined the Catlettsburg Church, but worshiped in their own chapel which was paid for by contributions from Louisville, Memphis, and Huntington, West Virginia. Congregations from those cities also sent clothes and other items for the "destitute" in Hampton City.[60]

Missions such as the one in Hampton City were common. Also frequent were new church developments in areas removed from already functioning congregations. The heartland church moved into all the state.

The Rev. William H. Sheppard (1865–1927), his wife Lucy G., and their children. Sheppard served the Grace Presbyterian Church in Louisville after having served with distinction as a missionary in Africa.

Typical Presbyterian session, 1949. These were the members of the session of the Versailles Presbyterian Church.

CHAPTER 8.

Into All Kentucky

All the elements fit together as the Presbyterians changed in their communal life. Revivals, program emphases, and long pastorates infused new energy and provided a sense of continuity at the same time. The formation of semi-autonomous organizations for women helped bring the talents of the majority of church members into the mainstream of its life. In the Cumberland Church, even the ordination of a woman took place, a radical departure from tradition.

Perhaps the most significant ingredient in the emergent heartland church of the PCUSA and the PCUS, however, was the increasing sense of mission. This evangelical spirit, a product of both revivalism and Christian nurture, had particular implications for the history of Kentucky Presbyterianism in its zeal to carry the gospel to all persons. Both the rural unchurched and the urban poor increasingly became subjects of concern in Presbyterian denominations.

As Presbyterianism had existed first in the Bluegrass area, so its self-perceived center remained tied at the turn of the century to the more affluent areas of the state. But its concern did stretch to include the whole population, especially in the Appalachian mountain region. Though Presbyterians did not move with full vigor to acknowledge the equal rights of black people in congregational and judicatory activity, they did enable viable and healthy churches, together with service-oriented centers, in behalf of the black population of Kentucky. This special and ethnic inclusivity not only helped a climate in the commonwealth which took seriously the educational and health needs of various kinds of people; it also enabled the Presbyterian churches to increase in number and in diversity of membership.

The colonizing efforts of local congregations naturally related to the efforts of presbyteries and synods to form new churches. In addition to the work of S. D. Boggs and other regular pastors who gave a portion of their time to the task of gathering additional congregations in nearby locations, various judicatories hired ministers on a full-time basis to serve as evangelists. The beginning of concerns for home mission issued from interest in foreign mission in both the PCUSA and the PCUS. In the PCUSA Synod, representatives of the various boards began making regular appearances to request people and money for their work—Foreign Missions and Home Missions. In the PCUS Synod, foreign missionaries themselves belonged to the body and regularly presented needs to their colleagues. For a brief time, 1874–76, the Presbytery of Hangchow in China was attached to the Synod of Kentucky.[1]

When E. O. Guerrant chaired the Southern Synod's newly formed Committee on Home Missions in 1877, the vision of what Kentucky Presbyterians needed to do in their own area was presented:

> Of the one hundred counties in Kentucky, sixty are entirely unoccupied by our church. Of the one million people in Kentucky, only ten thousand are members of our Church or one in a hundred.
>
> To give you an idea of the destitution of the country, in the regions beyond us, I need only tell you that in one day's ride from Mt. Sterling, the capital of eastern Kentucky, there are four county seats which have no houses of worship, and some of these towns contain hundreds of souls. They have jails and gambling halls, but no house for God's worship. And these people are anxious to have God's word preached to them. I had dozens of invitations and could have preached every day to these people. They are hospitable, as all Kentuckians are; more religiously inclined than most of them because less exposed to the snares of covetousness and ambition, intemperance and fashion. Having no advantages of an educated minister, they are exceedingly teachable. They love to go to church and turn out en masse whenever afforded an opportunity to hear one of our ministers.
>
> But . . . nearer home . . . In spite of the fact of great increase of population, wealth, general intelligence, morality and facilities for travel and commerce, the Church has stood still, or gone at best at a

> stagecoach gait, while the world has moved away on railroads, steamboats and telegraphs.[2]

During the 1870s, several seminary students received an apprenticeship in the mountains, paid with Synod's funds to try to open churches and schools among the Highlanders. The real stimulation of missions occurred in October 1881, however, at the meeting of Synod. Stuart Robinson had died one week before the meeting took place. His son-in-law, Bennett Young, together with a good friend and business colleague, Richard S. Veech, sent a telegram to the members of the judicatory.[3]

Young and Veech offered $2,500 each, if Synod matched it, to establish a concentrated evangelistic program in the state. The members of Synod immediately endorsed the plan, assured the laymen an equal sum would be gathered, and asked Guerrant to superintend the Synod mission in Eastern Kentucky. They also asked the Rev. W. D. Morton to be an evangelist in Western Kentucky.[4]

The work of Morton was significant, but that of Guerrant proved so pivotal for Kentucky Presbyterianism that it deserves special attention.

E. O. Guerrant

Born in Sharpsburg, Kentucky, on February 28, 1838, Edward O. Guerrant had been reared in a pious family of Huguenot descendants. His mother died in 1850, and his father a country doctor, managed to keep the boy in school while maintaining his small medical practice. Guerrant graduated from Centre College in 1860, and he entered Danville Seminary that fall to study for the ministry. Illness forced him to leave school and the Civil War intervened before he could return. Guerrant enlisted in the Confederate army and served as a military secretary for General Humphrey Marshall, as a captain under General John Hunt Morgan, and as Assistant Adjutant-General of the brigade.[5]

After the war, Guerrant studied medicine at the Bellevue Hospital Medical College in New York. He returned to Mt. Sterling, Kentucky, where he established what soon became a lucrative practice. He also married Mary Jane DeVault, from Leesburg, Tennessee and they had ten children.[6]

Convinced that he finally must enter the ministry in 1873, E. O. Guerrant left Mt. Sterling and attended Union Seminary in Hampden-Sydney, Virginia. There he became fast friends with Dr. Robert L. Dabney and several others who subsequently encouraged students to join in Guerrant's work.[7]

Upon graduation Guerrant began service in three small churches near Mt. Sterling—Salem at Pine Grove, Union, and Walnut Hill. In January 1876, he accepted a call to the Mt. Sterling Church itself. Less than three years later, he was called to the First Presbyterian Church, Louisville, as the portion of the congregation who went with the Southern Church sought to recover from the schism. In each of these congregations, Guerrant greatly increased membership and directed the people into avenues of mission. At the same time, he chaired for the Synod the Committee on Home Missions. He led that group in discerning the need for Presbyterians to attend to evangelism and social services right within the estate.[8]

Despite the protests of leaders at First Church in Louisville, Guerrant accepted the call and moved to begin the work. He focused many of the resources of the Bluegrass upon the needs of the Appalachian peoples. He would hire young men for a summer or a year and locate them in a town where a church could begin. He would preach in the wealthier churches in the state and journey elsewhere in order to raise money and enlist young people in the cause. He would write letters to those who could help in any way. Mostly, though, Guerrant would ride his horse into the "hollers" and small communities, especially into the county seats, and he would preach.[9]

During his first year, Guerrant led a revival at Richmond, where townspeople and students at Central University could gather. He then helped foster revivals in Lexington in late January, Harrodsburg in February, Bayless Memorial Church in Grayson and the Maysville Church in March. He finished work with the "organized" congregations with an April revival in Lebanon.[10]

In early May, he went to Salvisa with "Uncle" Joe Hopper, who led singing and helped in the baptisms. They found that one elder and a few women members still met for worship occasionally, but no pastor had been there for years. In ten days, "fifty-seven were added to the church." He located some men who would serve as elders, and he assigned a seminary student to meet with them during the summer. Soon the congregation formed a Sabbath school, too.

In late May, Guerrant and Hopper rode to Hazel Green, Wolfe County, and gathered forty-six to form a Presbyterian church there. In early July, Guerrant held a meeting at Irvine, the Estill County seat, and he re-formed a church that had ceased functioning for several years. He likewise organized churches at New Hope, in Nelson County, and at Comb's Ferry, in Clark County. He also visited several other locations—for example, Manchester in Clay County—but he declined to organize a church there because another mainline Protestant body already had begun work.

One young man who became a minister, in part as a result of Guerrant's appeal, described his appearance and effect:

> I remember how Dr. Guerrant came into the church, with his quick, elastic step, his erect carriage, his swift, all-inclusive glance. He was of rather less than medium height, but from the waist up was exceedingly well and gracefully built; his finely molded head was covered with a suit of raven-black, glossy hair.
>
> His features were rather large, but harmoniously arranged. The cheek bones were a little high, the nose large but well shaped, the lips full, the chin strong. He wore a rather heavy moustache, cropped "side burns" and a "goatee." It as a makeup was very becoming to him. The features, though, that you saw and remembered were his eyes. They were large, dark and at times quite black. They were exceedingly expressive as the lights in them would come and go, and they had the singular quality of giving the impression of seeing everywhere in the area and of looking every person in the audience, however large, directly in the face.
>
> The pulpit had been moved back and the platform extended. This strange preacher could not tolerate anything between him and the audience. It was long before the days of Billy Sunday and Sam Jones, and Mr. Moody was just beginning to be a large figure. The crowds filled the church night after night. The preacher was not only magnetic and compelling and unique, but, what was a complete innovation, he would accept no invitations but hurried away from the meeting to get to his room in the Commercial Hotel, which was next door to the church.
>
> I cannot recall now the number of professions there were during those thrilling days, but it was large. There was no incorrect speech, as was sometimes true in Mr. Moody's sermons, nor was there any coarseness, as with Sam Jones or Billy Sunday. There were, though,

> both humor and pathos, produced with a skill that mastered the audiences and never weakened the impression of deep sincerity.[11]

This account of the Harrodsburg meeting by W. O. Shewmaker highlights the rather "Confederate" appearance Guerrant maintained. He evidently accepted this persona with a broadcloth cape he wore that resembled a military greatcoat. Part orator and showman, part revivalist, and part a modest minister of the gospel, he fitted his sermons and meetings to suit the circumstances.

Guerrant's sermons, typically thematic, focused on things people knew from everyday life—"The Heart," "Laborers Wanted," "The Lilies of the Fields." He would make three or four points and usually end with a ringing, emotional call for repentance and faith.[12]

From time to time, Guerrant would indulge in the anti-intellectualism rampant in his day: "So all the scientific books might have told this man that miracles were impossible, and that blind eyes could not be opened! But he knew better. . . . " More frequently, though, he appealed to the better instincts and feelings—of sympathy, hope, joy in nature's beauty, and love.[13]

The ministry of E. O. Guerrant as Synod Evangelist lasted about four years, formally speaking. In October 1885, because his health frequently failed, Guerrant was forced to resign as the evangelist. He accepted the settled pastorate at the Troy Church and the new Wilmore Church, in Woodford and Jessamine Counties respectively. He still offered occasional leadership for revival efforts in Florida, Tennessee, Michigan, Mississippi, Alabama, and other states. His heart remained with Kentucky's mountain people, though, and he returned when he could to churches he had enabled to begin—Hazel Green, Beth Salem, Gilmore, Frozen Creek, Hazard, Troublesome, and the rest.[14]

On one trip, in the September of 1889, when Guerrant found the little chapel "on the Frozen, burned by some bad man," he grieved its loss. Later, he joyed in the improvement he saw of the community of Jackson, seat of "Bloody" Breathitt County. "Brother Mickel," (the Rev. Eugene P. Mickel from New York who succeeded Guerrant as Synod Evangelist) had built his parsonage right in Jackson. Again, as was his custom, Guerrant preached on the trip in homes, churches, and on one occasion, in a bar. He tried to get into the prison at the mouth of Twin Creeks, but he was denied access because the camp "was too full."[15]

Guerrant relinquished the Troy Church pulpit in 1896, and five years later he had to resign also from the Wilmore pastorate to devote fulltime again to what he called "The Mountain Work." From 1889, however, he and his family lived at "Belvoir," a home he built on a hundred-acre tract outside Wilmore. Guerrant himself planted fruit trees and ornamental shrubs, and the family kept servants to supplement their own work.[16]

As his fame as a revivalist spread, Guerrant sought increasingly to channel resources from the more affluent parts of the country into what he called "The Mountain Work." He began more pointedly to direct his words to a wider audience than Presbyterians alone. Seldom had he ever retreated to a parochial stance, and sometimes he had baptized Methodists or Baptists into other churches while a Presbyterian companion baptized the Presbyterians. But by 1897, Guerrant felt called to organize "The Society of Soul Winners: American Inland Mission." Through the society, people of all denominations could contribute to the schools, hospitals, and churches.[17]

Begun in 1897, as a personal enterprise in which Dr. Guerrant and a few friends hired one missionary to serve on the side of the Cumberland Mountains, the mission by 1902 supported sixty-seven evangelists working the Appalachian portions of Tennessee, North Carolina, Virginia, and Kentucky. Guerrant, as President of the Society of Soul Winners, raised money and published an eight-page monthly, beginning in 1902.[18]

On one of his trips East, Guerrant preached widely in New York City and in Brooklyn, including the church where the Rev. Harvey S. Murdoch served. Guerrant convinced Murdoch to come to Kentucky, to Canoe, which was a few miles from Buckhorn, for the dedication of a chapel that Murdoch's church paid to have built. Murdoch stayed as Field Secretary of the Society of Soul Winners, married Louise Saunders whose parents already served the mission, and together the couple established Witherspoon College in Buckhorn.[19] Built of logs and donated materials, the college served the special needs of the highlanders by offering a school for disciplined education without the usual, cosmopolitan accoutrements. To such an enterprise the people would send their children, and at the school the cycle of poverty could be broken while Christian training also took place. When a saloon-keeper sought to build and operate just across the county line, Murdoch evidently convinced the man of his error; the missionary bought at a bargain price the almost completed building, not to mention a stock of whiskey. The whiskey was destroyed, the building re-erected as a poultry house at Buckhorn.[20]

In his introduction to a book of Guerrant's sermons, Egbert W. Smith gave some of the statistics for the "Society of Soul Winners," which flourished under Murdoch's hand also:

> In ten years 362 missionaries employed by this Society labored exclusively in these wild mountains, holding over 22,000 public services at 10,069 places, reporting 6,304 conversions, teaching 879 Bible schools, with 39,500 pupils, distributing over 10,000 Bibles and Testaments, and 125,000 tracts, building 56 churches, schools and mission houses, including three Colleges and an Orphan Asylum.[21]

Other Evangelists and Efforts

As indicated, Guerrant did not work alone in the area of evangelism. W. D. Morton, selected in 1881 with Guerrant, took responsibility for the unchurched in the Western part of the state, Dr. Morton had been pastor of the Morganfield Church at the time. Though he only worked three years in full-time evangelism for Kentucky Presbyterians, he helped put in motion the considerable effort to have a church in every county seat town.[22]

A particularly effective evangelist replaced Guerrant in Eastern Kentucky in 1883—Joseph Madison Evans. Born in Nicholas County, Kentucky, in 1836, Evans had graduated from both Centre College (1862) and Danville Theological Seminary (1865). He had served congregations in Mayslick and Paris, Kentucky, before his call to Synod responsibility, and he remained in that work until 1917, when he moved to Texas.[23]

A lay leader who had worked with Guerrant was hired full-time to assist Evans. "Uncle" Joe Hopper, a ruling elder at the Perryville Church, led singing and Sunday school services when the Presbyterians would first enter a town. In 1884, the Synod commissioned Hopper to oversee the colportage work in rural areas. Subsidized copies of the Bible, of catechisms and Sunday school lessons were sold to enable a curriculum for the congregations and devotional readings in homes.[24]

The team of Evans and Hopper was a familiar one in all portions of the state. During 1886, for example, they went together to Mt. Sterling in March, to Somerset in April, where thirty-two joined the church, and to Lawrenceburg and Pisgah in May. They were joined by Guerrant in a successful effort to form a church at Morehead in June. They moved in turn to Franklin, Elkton, and Fredonia. The last-named evangelistic meeting was interesting, because at Fredonia especially the year before they had come at the invitation of a Cumberland Presbyterian congregation. They had reorganized the church and "set it on its feet" as a Cumberland Church. Thus they helped it along as they passed through the area.[25]

Young and Veech gave large amounts of money for at least two years, but gradually other individuals and congregations contributed more and more, enough to hire a whole group of ministers on a part-time basis.[26] Typically, competent and experienced pastors were given this responsibility, men such as Ben Helm, who had been a missionary for ten years in China, Robert E. Caldwell, who had spent an equal time as pastor of Highland Presbyterian in Louisville, and W. A. Slaymaker, who had been an evangelist in Tennessee.[27]

The work proceeded, and new churches continued to spring up across the state. The *Christian Observer* kept a running record of the events. At "Ford," Kentucky, where the Kentucky Central Railroad crossed the Kentucky River, Presbyterians began evangelistic services with Evans, Hopper, and Dr. L. H. Blanton leading them. At the end of three weeks, a church of forty-five had been organized, and they had raised $450 toward the construction costs of a building. A lumberman, H. C. Long, contributed some of the material; two other men sold a lot to the church "on reasonable terms."[28]

Scottsville, in Allen County, organized a church from a group of "five good women and one dear old brother who was acting as a ruling elder." Evans and Hopper worked to help organize what became in a short time a congregation of thirty-five. The sermons by the evangelists helped Methodist and Baptist churches in town, too, according to the account.[29]

The work of the evangelists had another effect also: "narratives of the state of religion," annually presented in presbyteries and synod meetings, became optimistic in tone. "Hopeful and encouraging" were the words the Synod used to describe the situation in 1886. E. T. Thompson, historian of the PCUS, described the evangelistic efforts in Kentucky as a "movement which soon spread through the Assembly, leading to a new era of missionary advance."[30]

The heavy emphasis upon PCUS missions in portions of the state previously neglected does not tell the whole story of Presbyterian involvement during the period. PCUSA and CPC missionaries also worked to establish new congregations and institutions. Most Cumberland Presbyterian efforts occurred in the south and west areas of Kentucky, and most of the PCUSA missions were in Appalachia.

One missionary, David Blythe, deserves a special word. Sent to Pikeville, Kentucky, where he served a small mission congregation, Blythe also initiated effort of the PCUSA to establish an educational enterprise among the mountain folk. The Rev. W. C. Condit of Ashland and the Rev. Samuel B. Anderson of Maysville cooperated with Blythe in locating land and support for Pikeville Collegiate Institute, begun in 1889. Blythe married Lucy A. Dobbs, one of the first two teachers working as the school opened under his direction. Pikeville College survived initial traumas, similar to those of frontier institutions in the Bluegrass a century before, involving rapid turnovers in leadership, lack of funds, and threats of disease. It became a stable and useful school during the first decades of the twentieth century, under the administration of Dr. James F. Record, who served as its president from 1899 until 1911, and again from 1915 until 1932.[31] Although the making of a PCUSA college in Pikeville was not an easy task, it became possible through cooperation of local supporters, gifts from congregations and individuals in the state, and help from the whole denomination.[32]

Not all the Presbyterian efforts progressed harmoniously, though, even in a denominational era of good feelings. George Barnes also went to the mountains in the 1870s and '80s. Barnes had been a missionary in India, after graduation from Centre College and Princeton Seminary. Upon his return to Stamford, Kentucky, Barnes had served a Presbyterian Church before Transylvania Presbytery took exception to his theology in 1871. As first a Darbyite and then a colleague of Dwight L. Moody, Barnes learned quickly and moved to become an independent evangelist himself. He healed and preached in Letscher, Perry, and Leslie Counties, as well as in the larger cities of the state. But the ex-

Presbyterian was seen as a threat to many of the churches in county seat towns as they struggled. The rumor circulated in Pike County that he had been "turned out" of Presbyterianism for drunkenness. In 1882, he moved the center of his independent ministry to Dayton, Ohio, and thence to the Northeast.[33]

Barnes and others worked in independent fashion. Their resultant congregations and institutions, when such were begun, for the most part remained tenuous and temporary. Some of those begun by the denominations were equally transient but others grew to serve people for decades to come. A few not only survived but indeed thrive, today.

Presbyterian Community Center

Black Presbyterians had been participants in local congregations since the early decades of the nineteenth century. Presbyterians had also provided some education for black people on an informal level for decades. But in the last part of the century, intentional Presbyterian "work" began among black people to help them form congregations and service networks. In 1888, for example, an evangelist was hired to work among Campbellsville's black population while he served as minister for a new "colored" Presbyterian church in Taylor County named the Praigg Church. A Presbyterian church also existed for black people in Bowling Green from about the same time. But few concerted efforts were made to evangelize and serve the poor blacks in Kentucky cities until the two missions arose in Louisville which came to be called the Presbyterian Community Center.[34]

That enterprise began when six students at the Louisville Presbyterian Seminary responded to a plea from the Rev. A. L. Philips, Secretary of Colored Evangelism in the Southern Church, to undertake a mission for the city's poor blacks. George V. Dickey, Edward H. Mosely, Edward P. Pillars, Hervey McDowell, Daniel Little, and John Little located a small dwelling on Preston Street, a store that had previously served as a lottery office, and opened a Sunday school there in February, 1898.[35] Twenty-three children came to the first Sunday afternoon meeting. The seminary students, all white, divided the black boys and girls, according to age and sex. Quickly abandoning the International Sunday Schools materials which they had begun to use, they developed personalized instruction more tailored to the needs of each class.[36]

What began as an experiment quickly became an indelible experience. The seminary students were impressed by the willingness of their students to learn, and by the "poverty of their wards." D. D. Little accepted responsibility during the summer of 1898 to maintain Sunday and Wednesday services, and he solicited volunteer help to provide teaching for the Sunday school classes. When they returned in the fall, the other five seminary students rejoined the effort; the summer volunteers, who were all women, remained; and new classes supplemented those still in progress.[37]

A boy from the "Smoke Town" area, South of Broadway, who participated in the mission, asked the seminary students to undertake work in his neighborhood. His persistence finally persuaded them and they rented a storefront in April 1900, to begin a second Sunday school. John Little kept both Sunday schools open that summer. In the fall, the independent missions became a part of the Presbytery's work. A committee, comprised of lay and clergy representatives, began to oversee the work. Judge Shackelford Miller, John Barrett, Wade Sheltman, and W. S. Macrea joined the Revs. W. W. Evans, G. V. Dickey, H. H. Sweets, and F. B. Converse to direct the effort.[38]

The committee employed John Little to superintend the Presbyterian Colored Missions." Little began to institute regular programs immediately. Already one sewing class had begun in November 1899, using a volunteer teacher and Little as her assistant. Now he solicited teachers for sewing classes in both locations. These classes quickly became oversubscribed, for they offered quality instruction and girls wore the fruits of their labors.[39] Miss Louise Speed and Miss Lucy Belknap, and other prominent Louisville Presbyterians spent large portions of their time in the teaching efforts. Miss Fannie Weller made substantial monetary gifts from the very first occasions of appeals for funds. They could not but be affected by the conditions they discovered:

> One Saturday morning while sewing school was going on I was called to a very destitute home and found a baby dead and wrapped in an old blanket. I reported it to the sewing teacher and when I conducted the funeral the baby was dressed in a dainty shroud that had been made on that Saturday afternoon in the sewing school. An old woman who had been a regular attendant requested her associates to make her a shroud

> when she passed to her heavenly home. The shroud was made and was so greatly admired that requests became so frequent that we had to decline to make any more because it was interfering with our instruction of the living.[40]

By April 1902, one mission had moved into its own building, at the corner of Roselane and Hancock. A partially-completed factory building was refashioned and turned into a mission and Sunday school. Thomas Grafton, a seminary student who came to work on the construction, also made a playground out of a small side yard. A sand pile, a large swing, and a wood contraption called "chute de-chute" constituted the only playground in Louisville available for black children in 1902.[41]

A Grace Presbyterian Church was formally opened for black people as a PCUS congregation. Subsequently a Hope Presbyterian Church was begun as a PCUSA congregation. In fact, the two community centers and their respective churches began and remained largely a cooperative enterprise among Kentucky Presbyterians.[42]

John Little, who led the Presbyterian Community Center for almost fifty years, maintained regular attendance at Second Presbyterian Church where his family belonged. In 1912 William Sheppard became the regular pastor of the Grace Presbyterian Church (PCUS). His presence as a respected black minister gave focus to the church, which became a center for black Presbyterian leadership in many areas of the state's life. A number of the wealthier black people in the community gravitated to that church under Sheppard's direction. Sheppard died in 1927, and his funeral in the Second Presbyterian Church afforded the first auspicious occasion for integrated worship among Louisville's Reformed Christians.[43]

The Presbyterian Community Center with its many activities helped pave the way for service and educational activity by the urban black population of Louisville. John Little, William Sheppard, and other leaders helped many of the urban poor to live in more comfort and hope.

Little was particularly fond of telling stories of those who had begun their education at the missions and had continued good works elsewhere. One was of a boy who saw a stereopticon lecture on Hampton Institute and decided to emulate Booker T. Washington. He had brought fifty cents a week to John Little, and by the time he could attend the school had saved fifty dollars. After graduation, he had served in the Army and then had begun an industrial school for blacks in Evansville, Indiana.[44]

The Presbyterian Community Center, and the coordinated congregations that grew around it, encouraged black people in other communities to consider Reformed Christianity. Thus the Louisville institutions became models for other, similar efforts. In the same manner, the inclusion of women in the Cumberland Presbyterian clergy began to open that possibility to other communions, but that story is even less well-known than the accounts of the Presbyterian Community Center.

Louisa M. Woosley

The extension of the Presbyterian Church into the whole of the state, and its ministry among the urban poor, received notice at the occasion of their occurrence. Presbyterians have taken scant notice of another extension of the church which occurred about the same time. In 1889, Louisa M. Woosley was ordained by Nolin Presbytery of the Cumberland Presbyterian Church. Her reception in the higher courts of the church could be generously described as "mixed," but her presbytery refused to require her demission from the clergy. Thus the ordination of a woman to gospel ministry stood, and partially as a result, in time the denominations all came to grapple with the issue that Louisa Woosley's ordination raised. In yet another dimension, Kentucky Presbyterianism spread—this time in terms of the sharing of responsibility for leadership between men and women.

Louisa Layman married Curtis Woosley in 1879. Born in 1862, and raised in a family of Baptists in Grayson County, she had experienced a call to ministry in her twelfth year. But her parents had encouraged her not to pursue formal education; they had reinforced in the family the cultural strictures on women assuming responsibility which almost all denominations shared.[45]

After marriage, Louisa Woosley tried to persuade her husband first to enter the ministry, "hoping" she said "to find relief by getting my husband to respond in my behalf." She failed in that attempt, and she undertook a "Bible search" on the matter. Despairing of an answer, she became depressed. She also bore two children; she felt that miraculous healing of one of her children confirmed her call to ministry. Again, after becoming exceedngly ill herself, she interpreted her subsequent recovery as a special work of Providence.[46]

In the Cumberland Presbyterian Church in Caneyville, to which she and her family belonged, Louisa Woosley was invited to preach when the regular minister was unexpectedly absent in 1887. She recalled that "for the first time in my life I went to the sacred desk and opened my mouth for God."[47]

Many in the congregation disapproved of a woman preaching. Others supported her in her quest to become a candidate for ministry, so many that she was received as a candidate by Nolin Presbytery in 1887, licensed a year later, and ordained in November 1889. She claimed that a number of congregations in the area sought her services, for special occasions and as a regular pastor. By 1891 she claimed also that more than five hundred people had been received into the Cumberland Presbyterian Church "under" her ministry. In that year she wrote a book on the topic *Shall Woman Preach? Or the Question Answered,* a thoroughly suffragist tract citing the biblical warrant for ordaining women and the work of many female professionals in various fields of endeavor.[48]

Louisa M. Woosley likely became the first regularly ordained Presbyterian woman in America, perhaps in the world. Her presbytery elected her as an alternate delegate to the General Assembly in 1893. The Assembly voted (85–78) not to seat her, as the Synod of Kentucky of the Cumberland Presbyterian Church had refused to seat her earlier. But no higher court sought to invalidate her ordination. Indeed several other CPC presbyteries received women as probationers.[49]

When Nolin Presbytery dissolved, the Rev. Mrs. Woosley was received into Owensboro Presbytery in 1899. The Cumberland Church also recognized a Miss Vianna Woosley of Leitchfield Presbytery as an elder commissioner, but it requested presbyteries not to send women as representatives to future meetings. For several years, the name of Rev. Woosley was omitted from court records. In 1911, however, the Leitchfield Presbytery restored the name of Louisa Woosley as a minister in good standing.[50]

Other presbyteries among the Cumberland Presbyterians began to ordain women in the 1910s, and by 1921 the General Assembly of the Cumberland Presbyterian Church acted to endorse the practice already in effect. The PCUSA in 1955 and the PCUS in 1967 followed suit. The Cumberland Church had also led the way in permitting, even encouraging, women to become elders.[51]

In addition, the Cumberland Presbyterian Church led the way in consideration of church union. That issue parallels the subject of evangelism in both time and significance.

CHAPTER 9.

Toward Union

In the twentieth century, Kentucky Presbyterians have generally followed in the patterns of work and worship previously developed—with one exception. Movements and actions in behalf of church union have become accentuated as time has passed. Kentucky Presbyterians have frequently been leaders in the efforts to unite Presbyterian bodies, as well as in broader ecumenical efforts.

Two institutional mergers occurred immediately at the beginning of the century. The united Centre College and the combined Louisville Presbyterian Seminary seemed to lead the way locally as Kentucky Presbyterians also did their share in the reuniting of the Cumberland Presbyterian Church and the PCUSA. While the Southern Presbyterians did not join in that church union, in Kentucky they did cooperate with the resultant PCUSA to form united, individual congregations. The Presbyterians in Kentucky subsequently voted for union of the PCUS and the PCUSA, a considerable effort which failed in 1955. Since that time, the cooperative endeavors of the Southern Presbyterians and the UPCUSA have been even closer than they had been previously.

To be sure, Kentucky Presbyterians have faced some new issues in the twentieth century. The place of technology in the church and its impact on the Christian life, historical-critical study of the Bible, and the regularization of vocations for non-parish clergy are just a few of the recent issues to touch the denominations. An unprecedented movement for civil rights for black people, a feminist movement of great force, a significant peace movement and the movement for responsible stewardship of the earth's resources have all been important for recent Kentucky Presbyterian history. Doubtless the nature of the denominations will change again as these matters comprise agenda for congregational and judicatory life.

The Cumberland Merger

In the first decade of the twentieth century another effort to reunite Presbyterians took place with sustained results. The Cumberland Presbyterian Church and the Presbyterian Church USA voted to merge. Although fewer than half of the members of the Cumberland Church in Kentucky actually joined with the PCUSA, they strengthened considerably the presence of that denomination in the state.[1]

The impulse for union of the two denominations stemmed from the willingness of the PCUSA to revise the Westminster Confession of Faith, a feat accomplished in 1903. A "Declaration Statement" also adopted, sought to provide a gentle, authoritative interpretation for the "hard" doctrines of traditional Calvinism—limited atonement, for example, and reprobation.[2] This formal softening of the Calvinism of the PCUSA led Cumberland Presbyterians to consider reunion with that portion of the Reformed family which had as they perceived it, repudiated "fatalism." Joint meetings of committees on "Cooperation and Union" took place during the fall and winter of 1903–04.[3] The committees considered the document upon which merger of the Old and New Schools had taken place in 1869. They used it as a model for the Cumberland-PCUSA reunion, except that the new basis included permission for separate racial and ethnic presbyteries should they be desired. The respective assemblies of 1904 voted to merge, a majority of presbyteries in each denomination concurred, and the assemblies of 1905 ratified the plan. The actual merger, finalized in 1906–07, enlarged the PCUSA by about 90,000 members. It provided for the first time numbers of white Presbyterians in the South for that communion.[4]

Recent studies by Hubert Morrow and John Ames have shown that another primary effect of the merger was that many liberal and evangelical Presbyterians were added to the PCUSA.[5]

By the same token, the reorganized Cumberland Presbyterian Church, which had continued into the 1900s with about 54,000 members, bore some resemblance to the church of 145,000 that had been led by those who merged.[6]

In Kentucky, where about 14,000 Cumberland Presbyterians comprised the synod, fewer than half actually joined with the PCUSA. Ames has determined that about 4,000 joined from the Cumberland Church in the PCUSA Synod of Kentucky in 1906. Others may have joined other bodies such as the PCUS and the Disciples of Christ. But the new presence of 4,000 more members in the PCUSA Synod meant a 50% increase in their numbers, for in records from 1905 the total membership numbered only 7,970. Statistically, the merger doubled the number of PCUSA congregations.[8]

Moreover, many new members and congregations came in Kentucky locations where few if any PCUSA churches had been located. Transylvania Presbytery, for example, received new congregations in such places as Swifton, Marrowbone, and Alum Springs. The Big Creek Cumberland Church in Adair County became the Union Church in 1912. Altogether a baker's dozen of new congregations joined the court.[9]

The presbyteries of Louisville and Ebenezer also gained a few congregations—in Fisherville and Calhoun, for example. But most of the new congregations were in the southwest portion of the state where two new presbyteries were established—Logan and Princeton. Logan Presbytery, with comparatively strong congregations in Bowling Green and Franklin, also included churches in Russellville, Auburn, and Smith's Grove. Princeton Presbytery, named for its urban hub, included congregations in Hopkinsville, Paducah, Mayfield, Sturgis, and Henderson. The experience in the town of Princeton itself may have proven exceptionally smooth. "A few months ago the session of the First Presbyterian (Northern) and Cumberland Presbyterian churches at Princeton, decided with hearty unanimity, that they would endeavor to combine their congregations . . . " one paper recounted. "The session of the First Church generously suggested that the pastor should be a Cumberland Presbyterian. . . . " The reconciliation there included the PCUS also, for it was determined that he also have oversight of a new "Collegiate Institution" which the Southern Presbyterians had just begun in the area.[10]

The presence of the former Cumberland Presbyterians in the PCUSA apparently did not affect seriously the attitudes of PCUS members in Kentucky. In the deeper South, the merger buttressed feelings of antipathy toward a reunion of the Southern Church with its denominational parent. In heartland Kentucky, though, cooperation did not diminish. The new PCUSA provision for a separate presbytery containing black churches, a result of the merger, resulted in the formation of a Lincoln Presbytery. The Louisville black congregation, called Knox Church in 1910, was grouped with the Praigg Chapel in Campbellsville, the small congregation organizing in Danville, and another in Camp Nelson to constitute a court of Synod.[11] On the one hand, such a segregated body reflected the Jim Crow racism of the day, separate but unequal jurisdiction. On the other hand, it afforded black people a more autonomous church environment in which to grow strong.[12]

Whatever the relative judgments concerning Lincoln Presbytery's life, the merger gave vitality to the PCUSA Synod of Kentucky. From 1907 onward, it could approach the PCUS Synod from a relatively equal position. Thrusts to stabilize struggling former Cumberland congregations gave a new sense of mission to the Synod.

United Institutions

In July 1901, the Synod of Kentucky, PCUSA, and the Synod of Kentucky, PCUS, agreed to merge all their major institutions of higher education. The Central University of Kentucky, as the united institution was named, consisted of Centre College in Danville, its recently initiated Law School, the Danville Theological Seminary, the Central University College Department in Richmond, the collegiate preparatory schools in Jackson, Elizabethtown, Middlesboro, and Danville, the Louisville College of Dentistry, the College of Law in Louisville, and the Hospital College of Medicine. A separate, though interlocking board of trustees, would oversee the merged Danville and Louisville Seminaries.[13]

Not everyone supported the merger. The redoubtable Bennett Young protested the removal of Central University from Richmond, Kentucky. The Reverend Taylor Martin from Virginia complained on the floor of the PCUS General Assembly that the union presented "a serious menace to the peace of the church."[14]

Over the protests of a few, the combined colleges and schools under Presbyterian direction got off to a fresh start. The catalogue for 1902–03, according to historian Hardin Craig, was "large and slightly pompous." It described a variety of programs and named all the faculty then serving. Dr. William Roberts was President of the University; the Reverend Lindsay Blanton, Vice President; J. A. Cheek, Treasurer; and Dr. F. W. Hinett, President of Centre College. According to Craig, several of the Central faculty were added to the Danville institution.[15]

Dr. Mary Ashby Cheek noted that "there was a gentleman's agreement to the effect that the Presbyterian Church, U.S.A. would have the dominant influence in the College of Danville with the President being customarily selected from that branch of the church. . . ." Gradually the various law, medical, and dental departments of the combined institution either ceased operation or merged into public institutions. The S. P. Lees Collegiate Institute later moved to become an independent junior college, and the unaffiliated Kentucky College for Women became a "Woman's Department of Centre College" in 1926.[16]

Historian Craig bemoaned the changes that transpired in curriculum, whether they came as a result of American democratization or of merger—the introduction of electives in various areas of study, the reduction in study of classics and classical language, and the twin "obsessions": specialization and departmentalization. What he decried most, educators would perceive as the necessary and healthy movement of the institution in the midst of an America increasingly complex and interdependent.[17]

Students, faculty, and administration began to gather again at Centre from diverse backgrounds and with widely varying skills, enhancing the measure of learning and proficiency in many different arts and sciences. Enrollment sagged a bit during the depression of the 1930s, but the school did not suffer inordinately.

Meanwhile the combined seminaries flourished well as a single institution. Members of the faculty rotated responsibilities for administration until Dr. C. R. Hemphill was chosen president in 1910. Subscriptions to an early financial campaign helped put the seminary on a solid endowment, and students began to come from various parts of the country.

Characteristic of the heartland church, seminary professors at the beginning of the twentieth century no longer received notice for their controversies so much as for their service.[18] According to the memory of J. Gray McAllister, a Professor of Bible, beginning in 1909, professors preached and taught throughout the area:

> Many churches in Kentucky were vacant at this time and the professors were busy from week to week in supplying them. I recall my extended service at Bowling Green, Frankfort, Shelbyville, Lexington, Paris, the last named for more than a year. There were also vacancies from time to time in the city and calls for other service on the part of the professors. Personally I have happy memories of the Pathfinders Bible Class, composed largely of teachers of Bible, classes from all over the city, which I taught at the Central Y.M.C.A. on Thursday nights through the last twelve years of my residence in Louisville. The professors did much work also at conference centers throughout the land.[19]

These two institutions—the college again named Centre in Danville, and the combined seminary in Louisville—represented the first institutional fruits of the new consciousness among Kentucky Presbyterians. No longer did many deem competition with other Christian bodies, especially other Reformed bodies, more significant than cooperation. Though Centre and Louisville Seminary did not receive direct benefits from other twentieth century actions toward union and merger, they did (and do) by their very existence support such a direction for Presbyterianism. Centre moved during later decades toward leadership independent of Synod direction, but in very recent years has reestablished a "covenant" understanding with pertinent courts of the churches. The Seminary remained and remains under both the PCUS and what came to be the United Presbyterian Church, U.S.A., the only such union seminary in the country.[20]

The movement toward union took place also at the basic congregational level. None of the remaining denominational attempts at merger thus far has proven successful, but the union of congregations has made Kentucky Presbyterians strive for greater union.

United Congregations

Among the new congregations in the 1880s and 1890s, it had not been an uncommon thing for PCUS and PCUSA to cooperate. Highland

Presbyterian in Louisville, as mentioned, had begun as a colony of both the College Street Church (PCUSA) and the First Presbyterian (PCUS). Founding members had come also from the Warren Memorial (PCUSA) and the Second Church (PCUS). Although Highland began and remained in the PCUS, it kept some formal ties with the PCUSA in mission and sentiment.[21]

It became a regular pattern for two congregations to merge amicably to affiliate with one or another Assembly. Thus, for example, the Southern Presbyterian Church in Mt. Sterling united with the Assembly Presbyterian Church, May 1, 1907. The united church became part of the PCUSA, but they worshiped in what had been the PCUS congregation's building.[22] The First Presbyterian Church of Paris, Kentucky (PCUSA) and the Second Presbyterian Church (PCUS) of that city merged in 1910 to become the First Presbyterian Church (PCUS). They gave some funds to Pikeville College, to the new church development of the PCUSA in Harlan, Kentucky, and the rest they used for the consolidated enterprise.[23]

Actual union of distinct congregations into union churches, aside from the denominational merger in 1905, began in 1913 with the union of the First Presbyterian Church, Harrodsburg, Kentucky, (PCUS) and the Assembly Presbyterian Church (PCUSA) of that community. The March 16 agreement was approved by the two presbyteries of Transylvania, and thus the United Presbyterian Church had its beginning. The Reverend M.V.P. Yeaman and the Reverend Bunyan McLeod, who had been pastors of the separate congregations, together served as co-pastors of the United Church.

Soon afterward, congregations in Lebanon and Shelbyville became United Churches as well. Others probably followed suit, for cooperation and union made sense to most Presbyterians in the state.

In the 1940s youth work became a joint enterprise between the two denominations. The Owsley-Lee Parish in eastern Kentucky was able to place six workers in several communities with a combined ministry. And in 1955, a joint office of Christian Education began its work in both synods.[25]

In preparation for a vote on denominational merger in the mid-1950s Kentucky union congregations such as those in Harrodsburg, Lebanon, and Shelbyville were asked to align themselves with one or the other communion.[26]

In 1954, the denominational union of three Presbyterian bodies was proposed. The United Presbyterian Church, with strength particularly in Pennsylvania and in the West of the United States, voted to merge with the PCUSA, who voted also to enter the union. The PCUS voted down the proposal in its presbyteries in January 1955.[27]

All of the Kentucky presbyteries of the PCUS, however, favored merger. Muhlenberg voted for it, 20–7; Lexington-Ebenezer, 35–16; Guerrant, 20–1; and Louisville, 97–0.[28] Their sentiments in favor of merger culminated in the formation of union presbyteries throughout the state, an institutional response accomplished finally in 1970. Union presbyteries enabled members to be fully participant in both denominations (UPCUSA and PCUS).

Kentucky Presbyterians worked with colleagues in other parts of the country to accomplish reunification of the two denominations.

Suburban Congregations

Another element in the drive toward ecumenism and Presbyterian reunion has come from the founding and growth of suburban congregations. Suburban congregations in the northern Kentucky communities around Cincinnati, in the smaller cities and Jefferson County areas surrounding Louisville, and even in Owensboro, seem to have been generally comprised of Christians with higher than usual rates of denominational mobility.

Particularly in Louisville, where a growing city invited the process of suburbanization, the strength of local congregations changed drastically as a result. Harvey Browne Memorial, perhaps the most obvious example, grew from a small neighborhood church to become the largest congregation in the state during the 1950s. People joined that particular church from a wide variety of backgrounds. The minister from 1949 until 1960, Olof Anderson, came to the church as an outspoken but gentle ecumenist. His openness to different types of piety and his enthusiasm for reunion among Presbyterians in particular and Christians in general characterized the whole church's program and mission. Each year through the 1950s the church grew by a hundred or more members; no sooner did a new building arise than it, too, became crowded with people in various activities.[29]

The suburban presence of Presbyterian congregations was augmented by the moving of some downtown churches to various outlying neighborhoods. Second Presbyterian of Louisville, a strong downtown church throughout the early decades of the twentieth century, began a part of its "regular" church in the vicinity of the Zachary Taylor Cemetery in 1950. Dr. William R. Clarke, Second's pastor, preached in a public school on Sunday afternoons for the suburban segment, until in April 1952, a majority of the congregation voted to relocate the church near Brownsboro Road. The new site, in the Rolling Field subdivision, received much attention from the church. A chapel with some office and classroom space was completed in 1955. A minority argued for maintenance of the downtown presence of Second, and they succeeded temporarily in staying a part of the migration.[30]

In February 1956, the downtown building at Second and Broadway caught fire and burned. An associate minister, Doug Chase, managed to save the pulpit bible and communion service. After this event, some members attempted without success to have a portion of corporate worship continue downtown. Vacation Bible Schools continued in the city until about 1960.[31]

Meanwhile, within the PCUSA Fourth Avenue Presbyterian Church, a similar movement took place with a different outcome. In February 1953, a steering committee noted that membership in the strong, downtown church had dropped by 25% in ten years, that 63% of the remaining members of the congregation lived more than three miles from the building, and that new property should be secured in eastern Jefferson County. A Real Estate Committee recommended purchase of about ten acres on Rudy Lane, and the congregation voted to buy the property in May 1953. A separate East Chapel became the Calvin Presbyterian Church, a self-sustaining and vital congregation. Fourth Avenue Presbyterian by 1956 became a part of a merged city congregation.[32]

The arising of strong, suburban churches in northern Kentucky, especially the Lakeside Church, also helped further union aspirations. Of course, suburban congregations had other effects on Presbyterianism as well. Meanwhile, Presbyterian institutions became less parochial and more thoroughly ecumenical as time passed.

A Common Witness

Presbyterians historically have perceived their responsibility as Christians to include ministry to the needs of all people. Thus they have sought to make common witness to the gospel, serving those in distress whatever their religious affiliation. They have cooperated with state agencies, where appropriate, to accomplish that purpose. The work of some Presbyterian institutions has been cited—for example, the Presbyterian Community Center and the Society of Soul Winners, which became ecumenically-supported organizations. The Bellewood Presbyterian Home for Children in Anchorage, the Cabbage Patch Settlement House in Old Louisville, and the Appalachian Regional Hospitals, Inc., are just three of the many other institutions which have served a whole population in meeting particular needs.

The Bellewood Presbyterian Home for Children began in 1853 as the Louisville Orphans' Home Society, with a facility on what is now called Kentucky Street. When Presbyterians divided after the Civil War, the property also was split. The Southern Presbyterians soon moved their orphanage to Anchorage, where they shared land with the Bellewood Seminary, a school for girls. In 1920 the PCUS Synod of Kentucky assumed responsibility for the orphanage which absorbed another similar institution from Springfield and purchased the entire tract of land next to the Anchorage Presbyterian Church.[33]

Early in its existence, the orphanage began to accept needy children who were not themselves Presbyterians and who did not come from Reformed families. The Bellewood Home, serving thousands of individuals over its 130-year history, cooperated fully with social service agencies of the state and with other denominations in its work. More recently, as ways of caring for neglected and troubled children have changed, Bellewood staff members have begun to engage whole families in therapy and have attempted to aid them in finding healthier ways to live.[34]

The Cabbage Patch Settlement House began as an independent Christian institution in 1910. Miss Louise Marshall, the daughter of Deacon Burwell K. Marshall and Elizabeth Veech Marshall, taught Sunday school at the Park Mission, an outpost of Second Presbyterian Church in Louisville. While still a teenager she was moved to establish a home for the destitute children in the Cabbage Patch area of town near the Sunday school. Her friends and their families, many of them comparatively wealthy, gave time and money to provide religious instruction, sports, sewing, arts and crafts, cooking, music, and other activities.[35]

In 1924, the Presbytery of Louisville adopted the Cabbage Patch, and its name was changed to the Ninth and Hill Settlement, but in 1929, the more commodious location on Sixth Street became its permanent home. Gradually, the relationship with presbytery became a less formal one, and the original name prevailed. The nature of the work, reaching people whom "the Church has never been able to reach," changed little over the years. Cabbage Patch remained a place of hope and learning, of refreshment and inspiration for the poor.[36]

Yet another example of the new common witness was the formation of the Appalachian Regional Hospitals, Inc., in the early 1960s. The Welfare and Retirement Fund of the United Mine Workers had established in 1955 and 1956 a series of ten hospitals in Kentucky, West Virginia, and Virginia to help the families of miners and others who lived in the coal producing areas. When the hospitals became a severe drain on the union's resources in 1960 and 1961, it threatened first to close hospitals in Hazard, McDowell, Middlesboro, and Whitesburg, Kentucky. The probability loomed, moreover, that all ten would cease operation.[37]

Presbyterians in the UPC, especially Dr. Kenneth Neigh and others in the national offices, cooperated with local pastors and governmental agencies to enable a private, non-profit corporation to assume responsibility for their operation. Though the Presbyterians had to confront suspicious critics and lobby for enactment of a bill in the state legislature, they persisted in behalf of the needy in the Appalachian communities. Edwin Stock, a historian of the events, pointed out that Presbyterians "acted boldly," not seeking to acquire anything for themselves.[38]

In these ministries and dozens of others—Buckhorn Children's Home, the Stuart Robinson School, Mt. Victory Academy, and Brooks Memorial Academy among them, Presbyterians have kept at the educational, health, and evangelistic ministries that needed to be done. Their history is both the story of that work and the story of their own life together.

Notes

Introduction: The Structure of Kentucky Presbyterianism

1. Among recent works on broader subjects, which include insights on Kentucky Presbyterians, are Walter B. Posey, *The Presbyterian Church in the Old Southwest, 1778–1838* (Richmond: John Knox Press, 1952); and Ernest Trice Thompson, *Presbyterians in the South,* 3 vols. (Richmond: John Knox Press, 1963–73). On the other side of the statement, such scholars as Harold Parker have traced particular, specialized topics. See Harold M. Parker, Jr. "The Synod of Kentucky, from Old School Assembly to the Southern Church," *Journal of Presbyterian History,* 41 (1963): 14–36; "The Kentucky Presbytery of the Associate Reformed Presbyterian Church," *Filson Club History Quarterly,* 46 (1972): 322–339; and "The New School Synod of Kentucky" *Filson Club History Quarterly,* 50 (1976): 52–89.
2. Notable among early studies were Robert H. Bishop, *An Outline of the History of the Church in the State of Kentucky, During a Period of Forty Years* . . . (Lexington: Thomas T. Skillman, 1824) and Robert Davidson, *History of the Presbyterian Church in the State of Kentucky* . . . (New York: Robert Carter, 1847).
3. Note, Thomas D. Clark, *Kentucky: Land of Contrasts* (New York: Harper and Row, 1968), pp. 120, 265, 272, etc. for just one example. One could not tell from the reading that Transylvania University had ever been Presbyterian, that Presbyterians debated infant baptism, or that the early revivals were ecumenical endeavors.

Chapter 1. Beginnings

1. Davidson, *History* . . . , pp. 1–53, 58.
2. An excellent description of the Scotch-Irish is offered by Guy S. Klett, *Presbyterians in Colonial Pennsylvania* (Philadelphia: University of Pennsylvania Press, 1937), pp. 26–36.
3. Davidson, *History* . . . , pp. 20–24; Thompson, *Presbyterians* . . . , 1:11–40, puts the same emphasis on "Back Country Scots," pp. 41–109, in a more balanced account of settlement.
4. Davidson, *History* . . . , p. 21.

5. Thomas D. Clark, *A History of Kentucky* (New York: Prentice-Hall, Inc., 1937), pp. 51–52, puts James Drennon and Hancock Taylor in the McAfee party. Lewis Collins, *Historical Sketches of Kentucky* (Maysville: Lewis Collins, 1847), p. 453, claims that it was McCoun, Jr., the husband of a McAfee daughter, who went, and has the McAfee party meeting another under the leadership of Taylor, as they floated the Kanawha.
6. General Robert B. McAfee, "The History of the Rise and Progress of the First Settlement on Salt River and Establishment of the New Providence Church," published in W. R. Jillson, *Tales of the Dark and Bloody Ground* (Louisville: C. T. Dearing, 1930), pp. 41, 42. See also *Register, Kentucky Historical Society,* 29 (1931): 3–16.
7. Davidson, *History* . . . , p. 60, does not name the servants. Collins says "Swein Paulson," p. 453. Willard R. Jillson, *Pioneer Kentucky* (Frankfort: State Journal Co., 1934), p. 93, distinguishes three McAfee stations: one, 1774 (sic) on the Salt River below Harrodsburg, by James McAfee; a second, very close to Providence Church, built in 1779; and a third constructed by William McAfee a mile west of Harrodsburg. The various stations are named in McAfee's narratives.
8. Collins, *Historical Sketches* . . . , p. 457.
9. Leonard Trinterud, *The Forming of an American Tradition* (Philadelphia: Westminster Press, 1949).
10. The first Kentucky settlers simply extended existing Virginia practices, although the number of slaves in the new area never reached those in the parent colony state. See Andrew Murray, *Presbyterians and the Negro* (Philadelphia: Presbyterian Historical Society, 1966), pp. 15–20.
11. William Whitsett, *The Life and Times of Judge Caleb Wallace,* Filson Club Publications, First Series, No. 4 (Louisville: Morton, 1888).
12. Ibid.
13. Thomas Marshall Green, *Historic Families of Kentucky* (Cincinnati: Robert Clarke, 1889), pp. 1–99.
14. Shane Papers, "Interview with Jane Stevenson," copy at the University of Kentucky. Draper mss, 13 cc, p. 35.
15. Bishop, *Outline* . . . , pp. 221–230. Davidson, *History* . . . , p. 69, gives another version of the history.
16. Charles G. Talbert, *Benjamin Logan: Kentucky Frontiersman* (Lexington: University of Kentucky Press, 1962), pp. 4, 258. A thorough reading of the minutes of the churches of Shelby County confirms this conclusion.
17. John Filson, *The Discovery, Settlement, and Present State of Kentucke* . . . (Wilmington: James Adams, 1794) in Willard R. Jillson, *Filson's Kentucke* (Louisville: John P. Morton, 1929), p. 29.

18. Bishop, *Outline* . . . . Other colleagues also suffer by comparison.
19. Davidson, *History* . . . , pp. 102–103. He used Bishop's *Outline* . . . as a major source.
20. The words are those from W. H. Perrin, J. H. Battle, and G. C. Kniffen, *Kentucky: A History of the State* (Louisville: F. A. Battley, 1887), p. 217. But the same phrase has been used time and again in Kentucky histories. See the argument traced in my "Terah Templin: Kentucky's First Presbyterian Preacher," *The Filson Club History Quarterly,* 53 (1979): 45–60.
21. Patricia Watlington, *The Partisan Spirit: Kentucky Politics, 1779–1792* (New York: Atheneum, 1972), p. 49, speaks of another ex-minister, Ebenezer Brooks, early inhabiting Kentucky. Brooks, who possessed an M.D., came from Delaware in 1781. He had been defrocked for heresy by the Leweston (Delaware) Presbytery. Brooks had become quite wealthy, in land holdings, when he died a bachelor in 1799.
22. Bishop, *Outline* . . . , pp. 62, 162–166.
23. Letter to Mr. Terah Templin, of Bedford County, Virginia, from Robert Carter, Nomony Hall, Carter Manuscripts, Duke University Library, Durham, N.C.
24. *Minutes,* Transylvania Presbytery (hereafter, *MTP*), I, p. 7.
25. See Bishop's tribute, p. 165. Also, W. T. Knott, *History of the Presbyterian Church in What Is Now Marion County and City of Lebanon* (Frankfort, 1895), p. 10.
26. Whitsett, *Life and Times* . . . , *passim.* Mitchel, Rice's son-in-law, has been generally omitted from the histories.
27. Ibid.
28. Ibid.
29. Bishop, *Outline* . . . , p. 66.
30. John Opie, "The Melancholy Career of 'Father' David Rice," *Journal of Presbyterian History,* 47 (1969): 295–319, gives one thorough account of his migration.
31. Ibid.
32. Ibid.
33. On Davies, see W. H. Foote, *Sketches of Virginia* (Philadelphia: W. S. Martien, 1850), I: 157–307.
34. Bishop, *Outline* . . . , p. 55.
35. Murray, *Presbyterians* . . . , p. 15, argues that it was the fact that Rice preached so much to slaves and with such effect, that forced him to take his family to the frontier. I cannot find the substantiation for such a claim.
36. Bishop, *Outline* . . . , pp. 72–110.

37. Davidson, *History* . . . , p. 73.
38. Ibid., p. 79–80.
39. Otis Rice, *Frontier Kentucky* (Lexington: University Press of Kentucky, 1975), especially Chapter 5.
40. Historians speak, however, of the well-honed doctrine of "fatalism" that many of the early explorers articulated.
41. Collins, *Historical Sketches* . . . , p. 23.
42. Bishop, *Outline* . . . , p. 26.
43. Steven A. Channing, *Kentucky* (New York: W. W. Norton, 1977), pp. 45–48.
44. Temple Bodley, *History of Kentucky* (Chicago: J. J. Clarke, 1928), I, Chapters 9 and 10, offers a particular emphasis on Clark's contribution.
45. Ibid., p. 532.
46. Quoted from McAfee papers in Collins, *Historical Sketches* . . . , p. 456.
47. Jillson, *Tales of the Dark and Bloody Ground,* pp. 3–5.
48. John Rogers, editor, *The Biography of Eld. Barton Warren Stone, Written by Himself* (Cincinnati: James, 1847), p. 26. Davidson, *History* . . . , p. 72, speaks of an ambush at New Providence.
49. Shane Papers, Interview with Robert Griffin. Draper Manuscripts, 13 cc, p. 28. (Microfilm available, University of Kentucky, Lexington, Ky.).
50. Collins, *Historical Sketches* . . . , pp. 40–69. As late as 1847, Lewis Collins still wrote without apology: "It was an established custom in Kentucky at that time, never to suffer an Indian invasion to go unpunished, but to retaliate upon their villages and corn fields, the havoc, which their own settlements had experienced." *Historical Sketches* . . . , p. 27.
51. Some ministers such as Barton Stone found "the weeds were getting ahead of my corn." Rogers, *Biography* . . . , p. 50.
52. Channing, *Kentucky,* pp. 44–47.
53. Daniel Drake, *Pioneer Life in Kentucky, 1785–1800* (New York: Henry Schuman, 1948), pp. 94–96.
54. Talbert, *Benjamin Logan* . . . , pp. 22, 201.
55. David Rice, "Slavery Inconsistent with Justice and Good Policy," in Bishop, *Outline* . . . , pp. 386–418.

Chapter 2. Organization

1. In 1800, *Minutes* of the General Assembly do indicate that 219 of 449 congregations in the U.S. had no pastors. *Minutes,* General Assembly, PCUSA, (Hereafter *MGA*), 1800. Clifford Drury, "Missionary Expansion

at Home,'' in Gaius J. Slosser, *They Seek a Country* (New York: Macmillan, 1955), pp. 165–190, considers the chief inhibition a difference of opinion on the expenditure of mission funds between ecumenists and denominationalists.

2. In a more complex study of Reformed Christianity in Kentucky, the contributions of particular Baptists and other such Christians would be explored. The lines between Presbyterian and Baptist were not clearly drawn in the period.
3. This formal statement has appeared frequently from Davidson, *History* . . . , p. 67.
4. Calvin M. Fackler, *A Chronicle of the Old First* (Presbyterian Church, Danville, Ky.), *1784–1944* (Louisville: Standard Printing, 1946) makes the claim, but general records do not sustain most of it.
5. Davidson, *History* . . . , pp. 73, 74.
6. *MTP* (1785), conference record.
7. Bishop, *Outline* . . . , p. 147; Fackler, *Chronicle* . . . , p. 18.
8. *MTP;* Whitsett, *Life and Times* . . . , p. 111, argues that this congregation was the first.
9. Robert B. McAfee, ''The History of the Rise and Progress of the First Settlement on Salt River and Establishment of the New Providence Church,'' *The Register of the Kentucky State Historical Society,* 29 (1931): 1–29. Even so, when Thomas Cleland became minister of that congregation in 1813, he lamented that the session maintained no records. Edward P. Humphrey and Thomas H. Cleland, *Memoirs of the Rev. Thomas Cleland, D.D.* (Cincinnati: Moore, Wiktach, Key & Co., 1859), p. 99.
10. Ibid.
11. Bishop, *Outline* . . . , pp. 223, 226.
12. *MTP,* I (1789): 30.
13. Julius Melton, *Presbyterian Worship in America* (Richmond: John Knox, 1967), pp. 28–42.
14. Ibid.
15. *MTP,* I, early pages of Volume I recapitulate the conference. See also Davidson, *History* . . . , pp. 73, 74.
16. *MTP,* I: 4–5.
17. The use of the Jeremiad in Presbyterian life has not received careful attention, but see Sacvan Bercovitch, *The American Jeremiad* (Madison: University of Wisconsin Press, 1978) for a profound general discussion.
18. *MTP,* I: 9.
19. Melton, *Presbyterian Worship* . . . , pp. 11–26.

20. Most of the American colonial composers were of German origin, however. See Henry W. Foote, *Three Centuries of American Hymnody* (Cambridge: Harvard University Press, 1940), pp. 124–164.

21. *MTP,* I: 15.

22. *MGA,* 1789, p. 11. The Assembly recommended "to him the exercise of Christian charity toward those who differ from him on this matter which is exercised toward himself."

23. But even according to Davidson, a critical reporter, Rankin denied that the dreams possessed authority over the Bible. *History* . . . , p. 91.

24. *MTP,* I: 66.

25. A small Presbytery of Kentucky was formed in February, 1801, embracing parts of Ohio, Tennessee, Illinois, Kentucky, and Indiana with three ministers and three elders present. *The Centennial History of the Associate Reformed Presbyterian Church, 1803–1903,* (Charleston: Walker, etc., 1905), p. 20.

26. William O. Shewmaker, *Pisgah and Her People, 1784–1934,* (Lexington: Commercial Printing, 1935), pp. 13–22.

27. Draper Mss. Vol. 14 cc, p. 136. See also Robert S. Sanders, *Annals of the First Presbyterian Church, Lexington, Kentucky, 1784–1959* (Louisville: Dunne Press, 1959), pp. 10–12. Permission was given by Transylvania Presbytery for a city church to be constructed.

28. *MTP,* II: 106–110.

29. *MTP,* II: 183–194.

30. Davidson, *History* . . . , p. 110. Calhoun served the Ash Ridge and Cherry Springs Churches on the Elkhorn River until 1799, when he returned to Staunton.

31. Campbell had already been in Kentucky and returned in 1795 to pastor the churches at Smyrna and Flemingsburg first. He also practiced medicine.

32. Allen died in 1795, after a brief ministry. Davidson, *History* . . . , p. 138.

33. Marshall also conducted a very popular academy. Ibid., p. 107.

34. Stuart wrote the "Reminiscences, Respecting the Establishment and Progress of the Presbyterian Church in Kentucky" for the *Western Presbyterian Herald,* (1837) which were reprinted in the *Journal of the Presbyterian Historical Society,* 23 (1945): 165–179.

35. Davidson, *History* . . . , p. 105. He named also Robert Wilson, John Lyle, and Samuel Rannals.

36. *MTP,* II: 230–232.

37. *Minutes, Synod of Kentucky* (hereafter *MSK)* I: 5–12.

38. *The Statistical History of the United States, from Colonial Times to the Present,*

introduced by Ben J. Walterberg (New York: Basic Books, 1976), p. 28.

39. Z. F. Smith, "The Great Revival of 1800," *Kentucky State Historical Society Register* (1909). Quoted the Number as 1880.
40. Typescript, Robert Stuart Sanders, "Churches of Transylvania Presbytery, 1786–1968, etc." Vol. 1, n.p.
41. *MSK,* I: 10.
42. John D. Wright, Jr., *Transylvania: Tutor to the West* (Lexington: Transylvania University, 1975), pp. 1–13.
43. Davidson, *History* . . . , pp. 65–71. Shelby and Greenup both served as governors of the state. Samuel McDowell, also among the trustees, may have attended also.
44. *MTP,* II: 193–200.
45. Neil H. Sonne, *Liberal Kentucky, 1788–1828* (New York: Columbia University Press, 1939), pp. 54–58, details the proceedings. More contemporary studies, such as *Protestants and Pioneers,* by T. Scott Miyakawa (Chicago: University of Chicago Press, 1964), pp. 29–32, accept the thesis of Sonne without investigating other interpretations.
46. Toulmin actually resigned because the legislature finally termed his election illegal. Wright, *Transylvania* . . . , p. 31; Sonne, *Liberal Kentucky* . . . , p. 59.
47. Wright, *Transylvania* . . . , pp. 31, 32, points out that merger terms favored the older school.
48. George Nicholas was also hired on a part-time basis for the Law Department and Samuel Brown and Frederick Ridgely for the Medical Department. Wright, *Transylvania* . . . , p. 39.
49. Trustees at first defended Welsh against student claims that he came uninvited to meetings of their debating societies, for example. He laughed, coughed, and made faces at the expression of ideas contrary to his own. But the trustees released him because they found he neglected his teaching and ridiculed other denominations. Wright, *Transylvania* . . . , p. 42.

Chapter 3. The Great Revival

1. John B. Boles, *The Great Revival, 1787–1805* (Lexington: The University Press of Kentucky, 1972), speaks in detail of the growth (pp. 185–186) and the new denominations (pp. 150–160). The classic study by Bernard A. Weisberger, *They Gathered at the River* (Boston: Little, Brown, 1958) uses considerable irony to describe the events.
2. Dickson D. Bruce, *And They All Sang Hallelujah* (Knoxville: University of Tennessee Press, 1974), pp. 123–136, who addresses the issue of class in detail. See also William G. McLoughlin, *Revivals, Awakenings, and*

Reform (Chicago: University of Chicago Press, 1978), pp. 98–140; Charles Johnson, *The Frontier Camp Meeting* (Dallas: Southern Methodist University Press, 1955), passim.

3. Trinterud, *Forming* . . . , pp. 122–165. See also various interpretations of its meaning gathered in Darrett B. Rutman, editor, *The Great Awakening* (New York: John Wiley, 1970), pp. 89–197.
4. Trinterud, *Forming* . . . , pp. 270–271.
5. William McMillan, *The Worship of the Scottish Reformed Church, 1550–1638* (London: J. Clarke & Co., 1931), pp. 190–209. "To many places during the 16th and 17th centuries Communion was only once a year, although the 'occasion' might be spread over two or more consecutive Sundays" (p. 191).
6. On Calvin's understanding, see H. Jackson Forstman, *Word and Spirit: Calvin's Doctrine of Biblical Authority* (Stanford, Cal.: University Press, 1962), pp. 29, 99.
7. William D. Maxwell, *A History of Worship in the Church of Scotland* (London: Oxford University Press, 1955), p. 172.
8. William H. Foote, *Sketches of North Carolina, Historical and Biographical* (New York: R. Carter, 1846), pp. 368–370. David Caldwell, John McMillan, and Joseph Smith, all products of the College of New Jersey, served as teachers for McGready.
9. *MTP*, II: 129–174.
10. A covenant with his congregation, quoted in Boles, *Great Revival*, p. 48. See also John P. Opie, "James McGready: Theologian of Frontier Revivalism" *Church History*, 34 (1965): 445–456 for an excellent analysis of his theology.
11. Johnson, *Frontier Camp Meeting*, pp. 30–39, details the events. He follows McGready's and McGee's accounts for the most part.
12. John McGee, quoted in Johnson, ibid., p. 35.
13. James McGready, "Narrative of the Commencement and Progress of the Revival of 1800," in *Posthumous Works* , edited by James Smith (Louisville: W. W. Worsley, 1831), I: xiv.
14. Ibid, pp. xv, xvi.
15. Catherine Cleveland, *The Great Revival in the West, 1797–1805* (Chicago: University Press, 1916) still offers one of the most thorough accounts of the events.
16. Letter from the Reverend George Baxter to the Reverend Archibald Alexander, Jan. 1, 1802, quoted in Cleveland, *Great Revival* . . . , pp. 71, 72.
17. Richard McNemar, *The Kentucky Revival* (1807; reprinted, New York: Jenkins, 1846), pp. 1–24.

18. Ibid., pp. 24, 25. McNemar's ordination was delayed for almost a year because of his suspected "Arminianism." Since McNemar joined the Shakers, and since the book appealed for others to do likewise, the description should be appraised with some critical distance.
19. Rogers, *Biography . . . Himself*, p. 24. *MTP*, II: 100–156.
20. An excellent composite portrayal is offered by Boles, *Great Revival . . .*, pp. 64–69.
21. Rogers, *Biography . . . Himself*, p. 38.
22. John Lyle, "Account of the Great Cain-Ridge Camp Meeting, August, 1801," from Lyle Diary, printed in Cleveland, *Great Revival . . .*, Appendix V, pp. 183–189.
23. Rogers, *Biography . . . Himself*, pp. 39–43.
24. Peter Cartwright, *The Autobiography of Peter Cartwright* (New York: The Methodist Book Concern, n.d.), pp. 44–45.
25. Lyle, *Diary*, pp. 183–189.
26. Cleland, *Memoirs*, pp. 40–45.
27. Ibid., p. 53.
28. Ibid., p. 54.
29. Davidson, *History . . .*, pp. 163–165, called it "too free communication of the sexes."
30. McNemar, *Kentucky Revival*, pp. 28–30.
31. *MSK*, I: 19–24.
32. *MSK*, I: 19.
33. McNemar, *Kentucky Revival*, p. 43.
34. McNemar, *Kentucky Revival*, p. 45; and *Minutes, Turtle Creek Presbyterian Church*, quoted in Edward D. Andrews, *The People Called Shakers* (New York: Oxford University Press, 1953), p. 73.
35. Davidson, *History . . .*, p. 202.
36. Rogers, *Biography . . . Himself*, p. 38.
37. "The Last Will and Testament of Springfield Presbytery," available in H. Shelton Smith, Robert T. Handy, and Lefferts A. Loetscher, *American Christianity* (New York: Scribner's, 1960), I: 576–578.
38. McNemar, *Kentucky Revival*, pp. 80–84. Andrews, *The People . . .*, p. 77. See also Julia Neal, *The Kentucky Shakers* (Lexington: University Press of Kentucky, 1977), pp. 13–32.
39. Andrews, *The People . . .*, pp. 80–82. The Reverend John Rankin later joined and became an elder in the South Union community.

40. William G. West, *Barton Warren Stone* (Nashville: Disciples of Christ Historical Society, 1954), pp. 53–109.
41. Alonzo W. Fortune, *The Disciples in Kentucky* (n.p.: Convention of Christian Churches in Kentucky, 1932), p. 50.
42. Davidson, *History* . . . , p. 161.
43. Lyle, *Diary*. . . , pp. 183–189.
44. W. W. Sweet, *Religion on the American Frontier, 1783–1840*, Vol. II: *The Presbyterians* (Chicago: University Press, 1936), p. 90, said he quoted the term "anti-revivalists."
45. *Minutes*, Cumberland Presbytery, (hereafter *MCP*), pp. 1–4. See *MTP*, II: 303, 304. Also received by Transylvania, transferred to Cumberland, was the Reverend James Haw(e), formerly a Republican Methodist.
46. *MCP*, pp. 9, 17, 25.
47. *MCP*, pp. 30–40. Portions of the *Minutes* are illegible, and the number cannot be determined with certainty.
48. Hawe, as a member of the Republican Methodists, did not follow O'Kelly in the Christian movement. See Roy H. Short, *Methodism in Kentucky* (Rutland: Academy Books, 1979), p. 2.
49. *MSK*, II.
50. *MGA*, (1808) (bound with other years), pp. 408–409.
51. Davidson, *History*. . . , pp. 190–263.
52. Ben Barrus, Milton Baughn, Thomas Campbell, *A People Called Cumberland Presbyterians* (Memphis: Frontier Press, 1972), pp. 50–104.
53. Ibid., pp. 105, 106. The Cumberland leaders retained the Shorter Catechism of Westminister and dispensed with the Larger.

Chapter 4. Border Conflicts

1. Lowell H. Harrison, *The Antislavery Movement in Kentucky* (Lexington: University Press of Kentucky, 1978), p. 2, offers an excellent composite chart of the state's population figures:

KENTUCKY'S POPULATION, 1790–1860

	Whites	Slaves	Free Blacks
1790	61,133 (83.7%)	11,830 (16.2%)	114 (0.2%)
1800	179,871 (81.7%)	40,343 (18.3%)	741 (0.3%)
1810	324,237 (79.8%)	80,561 (19.8%)	1,713 (0.4%)
1820	434,644 (77.0%)	126,732 (22.5%)	2,759 (0.5%)
1830	517,787 (75.3%)	165,213 (24.0%)	4,917 (0.7%)
1840	590,253 (75.7%)	182,258 (23.4%)	7,317 (0.9%)
1850	761,413 (77.5%)	210,981 (21.5%)	10,011 (1.0%)
1860	919,484 (79.6%)	225,483 (19.5%)	10,684 (0.9%)

2. *Idem,* and the data on free blacks in Kentucky Presbyterian congregations simply is absent. Some churches named a few as "colored," but others did not. Presumably, some did not even count black members on the roll.
3. On the institution itself, see Louis Filler, *The Crusade Against Slavery, 1830–1860* (New York: Harper and Row, 1960).
4. W. H. Averill, *A History of the First Presbyterian Church, Frankfort* (Frankfort: 1901), pp. 25, 49, 67, 68. The Rev. Eli Smith, the first minister, served the church for a decade, and when he left the church struggled to maintain its identity.
5. Mrs. D. F. Myers, *A History of the First Presbyterian Church, Ashland, Kentucky* (Ashland: 1954), pp. 1–5, 21. Initial elders were Robert Poage, George Poage, Sr., George Poage, Jr., James Poage, and Thomas Poage.
6. Mary L. Wilson and Florence Wilson, *A History of the First Presbyterian Church, Maysville, Kentucky* (Maysville: Session of the First Presbyterian Church, 1950), pp. 13–18, 23.
7. *MTP,* II: 240; III: 18. H. McMurtrie, *Sketches of Louisville and Its Environs* (Louisville: S. Penn, 1819), pp. 126, 134, 137.
8. Edward L. Warren, *The Presbyterian Church in Louisville, From Its Organization in 1816 to the Year 1896,* reprinted from *Memorial History of Louisville* (Chicago: H. C. Cooper, 1896), pp. 1–3.
9. Averill, *History* . . . , pp. 197, 198.
10. Ibid., pp. 198–201.
11. The education of the poor, with evangelism among them, of course, was the original purpose of the Sabbath school movement.
12. Averill, *History* . . . , p. 174.
13. James McChord, *Sermons on Important Subjects* (Lexington: T. T. Skillman, 1822), Sermon 1, pp. 9–38. The twenty-one sermons in the book, and the seven in another show a consistency in method despite the differences regarding the Bible. See *A Last Appeal to the Market-Street Presbyterian Church and Congregation* in a Series of Seven Sermons (Lexington: T. T. Skillman, 1818).
14. LeRoy J. Halsey, *Memoir of the Life and Character of Reverend Lewis Warner Green* (New York: Charles Scribner, 1871). Green, from Danville, sometimes preached at Shelbyville and Danville while he taught at Centre (1837–40). After moves to Hanover, Indiana, and Allegheny, Pennsylvania, where he taught in theological schools, he served as a pastor in Baltimore and a college president at Hampden-Sydney College; he returned as President of Transylvania and then of Centre. Since he moved from manuscript to extemporaneous styles of preaching, the sermons collected are probably from early worship occasions in the 1830s.

15. Averill, *History* . . ., p. 93, says Edgar was born in Lexington, Kentucky in 1793. Myers, *First . . . Ashland,* p. 15, quotes a source claiming his family moved to the state from Delaware in 1795. Edgar first served the Flemingsburg Church; he subsequently moved to Nashville to pastor First Presbyterian Church there.
16. The Session Book of the Presbyterian Church, Greenville, Muhlenburg County, 1823–1878, (typescript notarized, copy, provided by the session).
17. Cleland, *Memoirs,* pp. 129–134. See also Rogers, *Biography . . . Himself.*
18. Cleland, *Memoirs*, pp. 136, 137.
19. He also attended Princeton Seminary. "Nathan L. Rice," *Dictionary of American Biography* (New York: Scribners, 1935), XV: 244.
20. Rev. N. L. Rice, *An Account of a Law-Suit Instituted by Rev. G. A. M. Elder . . . Against Rev. N. L. Rice, Presbyterian Minister* . . . (Louisville: D. Holcomb, 1837).
21. *A Debate Between Rev. A. Campbell and Rev. N. L. Rice on the Action, Subject, Design, and Administrator of Christian Baptism* . . . (Jacksonville: C. D. Roberts, 1857), see especially "Correspondence," pp. 11–48. This was just one of the debates in which Rice participated. He also debated Salmon Chase and others on the sinfulness of slave-owning, the Rev. D. Blanchard on Universalism, and Baptists on several occasions.
22. John Breckinridge had been Senator for Kentucky and U.S. Attorney General under Jefferson. Robert also took responsibility for settling his brother's estate under adverse conditions. See Lowell Harrison, *John Breckinridge: Jeffersonian Republican* (Louisville: Filson Club, 1969).
23. Ellis Merton Coulter, "Robert Jefferson Breckinridge," *Dictionary of American Biography* (New York: Scribner's, 1929) III: 10, 11. The article on him in Alfred Nevin, ed., *Encyclopaedia of the Presbyterian Church in the USA* (Philadelphia: Presbyterian Encyclopaedia Publishing, 1884), p. 95, says he was converted at Frankfort, Kentucky and transferred his membership from the McChord Presbyterian Church to the Mt. Horeb Church in 1829.
24. *MGA* (1831), pp. 157, 185–187. *MGA* (1832), p. 314.
25. Records of the seminary show his enrollment, June–October of 1832 and his graduation in the class of 1834. Edward H. Roberts, compiler, *Biographical Catalogue of Princeton Theological Seminary, 1815–1932* (Princeton: Trustees of the Seminary, 1933), p. 70.
26. Robert W. Hartness, "The Educational Work of Robert Jefferson Breckinridge" (Ph.D. dissertation, Yale University, 1966), pp. 12–16.
27. He was appointed by Governor Owsley, reappointed by Crittenden, and subsequently elected to the post in 1851.

28. Hartness, "Educational Work . . . " (p. 90) says the attendance increased from 10,220 in 1847 to 72,010 in 1853. See also, "Denominational Education," *Southern Presbyterian Review,* III (1849): 1–19.
29. "Breckinridge Papers," Vol. 64, 1833, and Vol. 68, 1835, cited in Hartness, "Educational Work . . . , " p. 17.
30. Bishop, *Outline* . . . , p. 144. Historians have generally cited the comparative "humanity" in Kentucky slavery, but according to antislavery critics, floggings and murders of slaves occurred. Theodore D. Weld, *American Slavery As It Is* (New York: American Anti-Slavery Society, 1839), pp. 65, 66.
31. Harrison, *Antislavery,* pp. 2–4. Data from the analysis in Shelby, Oldham, Fayette, Bourbon, and Jefferson counties is available in the Louisville Presbyterian Seminary Library. That work will continue as time permits, in order to determine more about the socio-economics of the Reformed bodies and their patterns of dispositional piety.
32. Robert P. Allen, Alexander Logan, Samuel Harbison, Singletary Wilson, and Charles Baird.
33. Mark Hardin. Wills for Thomas Norton and David B. Allen could not be located.
34. William Allen, Zechariah Bell, Alexander Logan, Henry Wiley, and C. Offutt.
35. *Willbook,* 10: 187, Shelby County, Kentucky. See *Minutes,* Shelbyville Presbyterian Church, for the lists. See also "Presbyterians in Shelby County," in George L. Willis, *History of Shelby County, Kentucky* (Louisville: C. T. Dearing for Shelby County Geneological-Historical Committee, 1929), pp. 93–98.
36. *Willbook,* 21: 144, Shelby County.
37. Sanders, *Annals,* pp. 105, 106. Maxwell's will located in *Willbook* L: 299, Fayette County, Kentucky.
38. *Willbook, N:* 231. Fayette County.
39. *Willbook,* L: 299. Fayette County.
40. *Willbook,* X: 596. Fayette County.
41. *Willbook,* O: 203. Fayette County.
42. *Willbook,* X: 596. Fayette County. The will of James Blythe, minister at Pisgah and supply at Lexington, First, left one slave after his death. *Willbook,* R: 458, Fayette County.
43. *Willbook*, F: 37. Bourbon County.
44. A thorough history of the Kentucky years is provided in Larry G. Willey, "The Rev. John Rankin: Early Ohio Antislavery Leader," (Ph.D. disserta-

tion, University of Iowa, 1976), pp. 1–36.

45. "Life of John Rankin Written by Himself in His Eightieth Year." Copies are available in Ohio Historical Society Library, Columbus, Ohio, and at the Public Library in Ripley, Ohio.

46. Rankin, "Life," pp. 1–12. Asa E. Martin, *The Antislavery Movement in Kentucky Prior to 1850* (Louisville: Standard Printing, 1918), pp. 12–17.

47. Thompson, *Presbyterians* . . . , I: 326–28.

48. Willey, "The Rev. John Rankin . . ." pp. 22–27.

49. Minutes of Ebenezer Presbytery, quoted extensively in Willey, "The Rev. John Rankin . . . ," p. 24.

50. *MSK* 5 (1833): 31. After the vote, Robert J. Breckinridge, a leader in antislavery, left the hall, saying "God has left you, and I also will now leave you. . . ." Reported in Hambleton Tapp, "The Slavery Controversy Between Robert Wickliffe and Robert J. Breckinridge," *Filson Club Historical Quarterly* 19 (1945): 163.

51. *MSK* 5 (1834): 50, 51.

52. Ibid., p. 52.

53. P. J. Staudenraus, *The African Colonization Movement, 1816–1865* (New York: Columbia, 1961) gives a thorough history of the enterprise. My article, "John Holt Rice and the American Colonization Society," *Journal of Presbyterian History* 46 (1968): 26–41, shows its impact on Virginia churches.

54. *MGA* (1818): 692.

55. *African Repository,* 6: 80, quoted in Martin, *Antislavery* . . . , p. 53.

56. Ibid., "The Colonization Movement in Kentucky—1816–1850," pp. 49–62. The major fight for leadership occurred between Robert Breckinridge and Robert Wickliffe, the largest slaveowner in the state, who wanted the Society to focus on sending free blacks and to refrain from interfering in relationships between masters and slaves.

57. Staudenraus, *African Colonization* . . . , passim, repeats objections of freed people and follows several of the riots which occurred in the process.

58. Fascinating was the fact that Crowe managed to remain in Shelby County, which as indicated was a center of Presbyterian (and other) slavery. He moved subsequently to found Hanover College in Indiana. See L. C. Rudolph, *Hoosier Zion* (New Haven: Yale, 1963), pp. 182, 183 for one account of the results.

59. There were 150 delegates in all. See Harrison, *Antislavery* . . . , p. 56.

60. On Birney's life, see William Birney, *James G. Birney and His Times* (New York: Appleton, 1890).

61. Birney, popular in the North as a lecturer and abolitionist, received the

1840 and 1844 nominations for President from the newly-formed Liberty Party, the predecessor of the Republican Party.

62. That is, the local church could determine its own covenants and regulations.

63. Fee minced no words. His *Non-Fellowship with Slaveowners* (New York: John A. Gray, 1855), said that "the sin of mystic Babylon, there, was slaveowning; and God commands his people to come out from such a church . . . " (p. 9). When he said such things in public, he was almost killed on several occasions. See Robert K. Loesch, "Kentucky Abolitionist: John Gree Fee" (Ph.D. dissertation, Hartford Seminary Foundation, 1969); see also *Autobiography of John G. Fee* (Chicago: National Christian Association, 1891) for accounts.

64. Samuel Hopkins, *The System of Doctrines Contained in Divine Revelation, Explained and Defended* . . . (Boston: Lincoln and Edmunds, 1811), I: 470.

65. Samuel Hopkins, *A Dialogue Concerning the Slavery of the Africans, Showing It to Be the Duty and Interest of the American Colonies to Emancipate All the African Slaves* . . . (1776). Available in Hopkins' *Timely Articles on Slavery* (1854; reprinted, Miami: Mnemosyne Pub., 1969).

66. One good exposition of the Old School perspective, from within the Princeton camp, was offered by A. A. Hodge, *The Life of Charles Hodge* (London: T. Nelson, 1881), chapter VIII, pp. 285–309. Also see John O. Nelson, "The Rise of the Princeton Theology," (Ph.D. dissertation, Yale University, 1935).

67. Charles Hodge, "Introductory Lecture, Delivered Nov. 7 in the Theological Seminary at Princeton, 1828," in *Biblical Repertory* 5 (1829): 92.

68. Scholars are divided on the question, "How vital was the antislavery issue as a cause for division?" Thompson, *Presbyterians,* I: 377–394, implies that the issue was extremely important. George M. Marsden, *The Evangelical Mind and the New School Presbyterian Experience* (New Haven: Yale University Press, 1970), p. 103, argues that "slavery remained one of the most frustrating of the many problems that beset the evangelical cause." In Appendix I, pp. 250, 251, he gathered "Historiography of the Causes of the Division of 1837–39; Doctrine or Slavery."

69. Of course, in the New School itself opinion was divided on both issues.

70. *MSK,* IV (1827): 21.

71. Ibid., pp. 21–24.

72. *MSK,* IV (1828): 31.

73. Ibid., p. 61.

74. *MTP,* V (1829): 96, 97.

75. *Minutes, Muhlenburg Presbytery* (MMP), I (1829): 60.

76. *MSK,* IV: 167–211.
77. *MSK,* IV: 226–236.
78. *Idem,* especially pp. 230, 231.
79. See Thompson, *Presbyterians . . . ,* I: 377–385, for both a summary and an analysis of the document.
80. *MSK,* V: 55–65.
81. Stuart Henry, *Unvanquished Puritan: A Portrait of Lyman Beecher* (Grand Rapids: Eerdmans, 1973), Chapters XII and XIII, pp. 207–246, offers a well-developed history of the case.
82. *MSK,* V: 80–85.
83. *MGA,* (1837): 580–588.
84. *MSK,* V (1837): 93, 98, 100.
85. Ibid., pp. 79, 98, 114–116.
86. Marsden, *Evangelical Mind . . . ,* p. 64.
87. R. S. Sanders, *Presbyterianism in Versailles and Woodford County, Kentucky* (Louisville: Dunne Press, 1963), p. 133.
88. Harold Parker, "The New School Synod," *Filson Club History Quarterly,* 50 (1976): 52–89.
89. Ibid., p. 57.
90. Davidson, *History . . . ,* pp. 358–361.
91. Parker, "New School Synod . . . ," p. 59.
92. See Thompson, *Presbyterians . . . ,* I: 406–588.
93. Davidson, *History . . . ,* p. 354.
94. Harold Parker, "A School of the Prophets at Maryville," *Tennessee Historical Quarterly* 34 (1975): 72–90, speaks of the other alternative in Northern Tennessee, under Dr. Isaac Anderson, a strong New School leader.
95. It was in 1857 that the New School split along regional lines, but the Kentuckians did not even make it to the meeting to form the New School (South) denomination. Parker, "New School . . . ," p. 82.

Chapter 5. Civil War

1. E. Merton Coulter, *The Civil War and Adjustment in Kentucky* (Chapel Hill: University of North Carolina Press, 1926), p. 30; Carl Degler, *The Other South* (New York: Harper and Row, 1974).
2. On John Cabell Breckinridge, see Frank H. Heck, *Proud Kentuckian: John C. Breckinridge, 1821–1875* (Lexington: University Press of Kentucky, 1976).

3. *MGA* (Old School) (1860), passim.
4. Cumberland Presbyterians resisted the gathering of data, and the actual numbers of communicants and churches cannot be discerned. None of the Kentucky presbyteries, with the exception of "Kentucky Presbytery," made reports in 1860. Kentucky reported 1100 communicants, but Logan, Cumberland, and Obion (part in state) gave no word. *Minutes, Cumberland Presbyterian Church* (1860), pp. 75–78.
5. *MGA* (Old School) (1860): 499–505. Apparently Kentucky ranked eighth in its numbers in synod that year.
6. *MGA* (Old School) (1861): 339–341.
7. Thompson, *Presbyterians* . . . , I: 566–571.
8. *MSK,* VIII: 45–51.
9. *MSK,* VIII: 82.
10. *MSK,* VIII: 94–98.
11. *MSK,* VIII: 98–112.
12. Glenn Clift, editor, *The Private War of Lizzie Hardin* (Frankfort: Kentucky Historical Society, 1963), pp. 64, 65.
13. Ibid., pp. 80, 81.
14. R. S. Sanders, *Presbyterianism in Paris and Bourbon County, Kentucky, 1786–1961* (Paris, Ky.: First Presbyterian Church, 1961), p. 26, shows a minute settling the claim against the Federal government, dates February 11, 1916. See *MSK,* VIII: 113.
15. Robert E. McDowell, *City of Conflict: Louisville in the Civil War* (Louisville: Civil War Round Table, 1962), pp. 44–131.
16. Ibid., pp. 145–148.
17. Indeed, the results in politics showed mostly confusion and dissipation of energies. In the 1860 election, Kentucky voters gave the plurality of votes (45%) to John Bell of Tennessee, a sizable vote (17.5%) to Stephen Douglas, about 1% to Lincoln, and only 36.5% to John C. Breckinridge, Vice President, and Robert's nephew. See Heck, *John C. Breckinridge,* p. 91.
18. Coulter, *Civil War* . . . , p. 27.
19. Robert J. Breckinridge, "Our Country—Its Peril—Its Deliverance," in *Danville Quarterly Review,* I (1861): 73–115, esp. 93.
20. Thomas E. Peck, *A Memorial of the Life and Labors of the Rev. Stuart Robinson,* pamphlet reprinted from the *Southern Presbyterian Review* (Columbia, S.C.: 1882), pp. 1–6. Robinson's mother died when the boy was young, and his father's infirmities had forced the "adoption."
21. Stuart Robinson, *The Church of God as an Essential Element of the Gospel, and the Idea, Structure and Functions Thereof, with an Appendix Showing*

the More Important Symbols of Presbyterian Church Government, Historically Arranged and Illustrated (Philadelphia: Joseph M. Wilson, 1858), pp. 25–114.

22. Ibid., p. 28.
23. Ibid., pp. 87–88.
24. Lewis G. VanderVelde, *The Presbyterian Churches and the Federal Union, 1861–1869* (Cambridge: Harvard University Press, 1932) offers a delightful sketch of both men.
25. On the differences, see Jack P. Maddex, "From Theocracy to Spirituality: the Southern Presbyterian Reversal on Church and State," *Journal of Presbyterian History* 54 (1976): 438–452.
26. News items concerning this period have been collected and are available in a scrapbook, (hereafter called *Scrapbook II*) by Alithea Brigham, n.d., in possession of Mr. J. V. Norman, Jr., of Louisville. Many of the items bear no date or identification of the newspaper. Robinson also became immediately embroiled in a controversy with the Unitarian pastor in Louisville, John H. Heywood, over the latter's right to address the YMCA.
27. Thompson, *Presbyterians . . .*, I: 564–571 follows the contest closely.
28. VanderVelde, *Presbyterian Churches . . .*, pp. 191–194. Robinson evidently managed to have amended a more one-sided endorsement of Breckinridge by threatening to resign himself if a tempered statement was not forthcoming. Both claimed victory after the fray.
29. Coulter, "Breckinridge," pp. 10–11.
30. Carl Sandburg, *Abraham Lincoln: The War Years* III (V) (New York: Schribner's, 1945), pp. 78, 79, provides an intimate, and presumably accurate, account of the incident: "The white-haired, bearded, and grizzled preacher took the platform while the roof rang with cheers for the 'Old War Horse of Kentucky.' "
31. The seminary had 3 students in 1861–62, 6 in 1862–63, and 1863–64, 5 in 1864–65, and 2 in 1865–66. Almost all were from Kentucky. It showed no students present in 1866–67. "Danville Theological Seminary Matriculation Book, 1853–1901," in Archives of Louisville Presbyterian Seminary.
32. Biographer Thomas Peck has pointed out that Robinson's stand simply upheld a position he had long maintained; Peck cited the separationist arguments Robinson voiced between church and state while in Frankfort. Peck, *Memorial,* p. 14. Lewis G. VanderVelde, *Presbyterian Churches . . .*, pp. 172–174, claims that Robinson himself edited more than two-thirds of the issues. Robinson had good reason to worry about incarceration. A Baptist publisher named Duncan was jailed. See Robert E. McDowell, *City of Conflict,* p. 74.

33. William Fleming, "Diary, 1861–1866," unpublished, excerpts loaned by Mrs. John Green, Louisville, Kentucky.
34. Robinson's sermons and lectures, with an organized choir to augment worship, Fleming remembered fondly. He recorded several occasions in diary entries when the Mechanics Institute Hall was full to overflowing.
35. Stuart Robinson, *Mosaic Slavery* (Toronto: Rollo and Adams, 1865). This, then, was one of the few pro-slavery tracts from "Kentucky," in Canada.
36. He maintained this willingness, remained consonant with his doctrine of the "spirituality of the church."
37. Numbers of clippings from Canadian papers, as well as from those in the U.S., attest to the notoriety of the discourses and book. *Scrapbook II*: 30–36.
38. Stuart Robinson, *Discourses of Redemption as Revealed at Sundry Times and in Diverse Manners* (Toronto: Rollo and Adams, 1866). Subsequent editions by the Presbyterian Board of Publication, Richmond, Va.
39. This may have accounted in part for its acceptance. Numerous reviews give evidence that the book received good publicity.
40. Robinson, *Discourses* . . . , esp. pp. 37–56. He also argued the priority of evangelism over ethics, pp. 251–268.
41. Robinson, "The Infamous Perjuries of the Bureau of Military Justice Exposed," a Letter of Rev. Stuart Robinson to Hon. Mr. Emmons, p. 2. Cf. "Testimony of Sandford Conover, et al. before Military Court at Washington . . . " (Toronto: Published as a pamphlet, 1865), p. 15. (Loaned by Mr. J. V. Norman.)
42. Robinson, "Infamous Perjuries . . . , " pp. 1–8. Robinson claimed that he had incurred Speed's wrath by "exposing the infidelity of Unitarianism . . . " in the Kentucky Senate in 1862 (p. 2), *Scrapbook II*.
43. Ibid., p. 8.
44. Hoyt, who only arrived in Louisville in 1859, later served as Moderator of the PCUS, in 1880, when he was pastor of First Presbyterian, Nashville, Tennessee. Wilson, the son of Joshua Wilson who had fought Lyman Beecher, vacillated between the two Assemblies during his later ministry. Scott, *Ministerial Directory of the Presbyterian Church, U.S., 1861–1941* (Austin, Tex.: Press of Von Boeckmann-Jones, for the General Assembly, 1942), pp. 334, 785.
45. VanderVelde, *Presbyterian Churches* . . . , p. 188. He provided the felicitous understatement: "From the outset of the trouble it had been apparent that the least tractable of Kentucky Presbyterians were to be found in the Presbytery of Louisville."
46. *MGA*, (1864): 277–325.
47. VanderVelde, *Presbyterian Churches* . . . , pp. 202–210 quotes exten-

sively from it. A copy of the pamphlet is available at the Louisville Presbyterian Seminary Library.

48. Ibid., pp. 5–17. An excellent analysis of the document is found in Harold Parker, "The Synod of Kentucky: from Old School Assembly to the Southern Church," *Journal of Presbyterian History,* (1963): 14–36.
49. Ibid., pp. 16–22. One could read the Old School "Act and Testimony" as similar in its argument.
50. *MSK,* VIII (1865): 154, 156.
51. Ibid., p. 164.
52. According to tradition, Robinson had even cooperated with Wilson in the writing of the "Declaration and Testimony against the Erroneous and Heretical Doctrines and Practices which have obtained and been propagated in the Presbyterian Church in the United States during the last five years," *MLP,* 1865, available at Louisville Presbyterian Theological Seminary.
53. VanderVelde, *Presbyterian Churches . . . ,* pp. 220–261.
54. Ibid., pp. 251–252.
55. *MSK,* VIII: 202–207.
56. Ibid., pp. 214–216.
57. It is fascinating that the minutes reflected the entire proceedings, including what loyalists perceived the "spurious" roll-call.
58. Barrus, et al., *A People . . . ,* p. 129.
59. Ibid., p. 138.
60. McDonnold, *History of the Cumberland Presbyterian Church* (Nashville: Board of Publications of the Cumberland Presbyterian Church, 1899), pp. 215–228.
61. Barrus, et al., *A People . . . ,* pp. 142–144.
62. This insight was suggested by Dr. John Ames, whose study of Cumberland Presbyterians will be followed in Chapter 9. See *Minutes, General Assembly,* 1862–1865, where each year the empty roll simply indicated that some who should be in attendance were absent.
63. Barrus, et al., *A People . . . ,* pp. 151–165. Certain synods, as for example in Ohio, did make more condemnatory statements of the Southerners. By the same token, Southerners did flirt with the possibility of organizing their own branch of the church.
64. *Minutes, General Assembly, CPC* (1869), pp. 32, 33. The report still bemoaned that "many of the Synods have failed to forward their records."
65. I have not had opportunity to review minutes of the Colored Cumberland Presbyterian Church. See McDonnold, *History . . . ,* pp. 432–439.

Chapter 6. Reconstruction Alignments

1. VanderVelde, *Presbyterian Churches . . .*, pp. 261–264. An excellent history of the process has also been provided by Harold Parker, "The Synod of Kentucky," pp. 14–36.
2. *MSK*, (Independent) (1866): 19–20.
3. See Lefferts Loetscher, *The Broadening Church* (Philadelphia: University of Pennsylvania Press, 1954), Chapt. 1 "The Wedding Day." The Princeton Seminary leaders, as well as Cyrus McCormick and some other lay leaders, had sought Old School union with the Southern Church first (p. 6).
4. See Harold M. Parker, Jr., "Much Wealth and Intelligence: The Presbytery of Patapsco," *Maryland Historical Magazine* 60 (1965): 24–38, for a good account of the events.
5. *MGA*, (PCUS, 1869): 371–74, 439–43. A parallel movement in Missouri was taking place, though not so forcefully.
6. Parker, "Synod of Kentucky. . . ," wisely used Assembly statistics for 1875, which allowed time for the demographic change to be reflected.
7. In another extremely important case, Danville Seminary and Centre College had been declared PCUSA institutions.
8. Van Dyke particularly inculcated the good will of the PCUSA, for he had stood with the Old School Southern contingent. For biographies of all three delegates, see Nevin, *Encyclopaedia . . .*, pp. 47, 192, 971, 972. On the Louisville Assembly, see *MGA* (PCUS 1870): 516, 517.
9. Warren, *The Presbyterian Church in Louisville*, p. 11.
10. In actuality, a Third Presbyterian Church had been founded by presbytery in May 1832, but it became "scattered" in 1836. Whether it was reorganized in that year, or whether another congregation altogether took the same name, cannot be determined from the texts. The "Minutes" of the Session of the Walnut Street Presbyterian Church, *(MWS)* begin only in 1857. Alternatively, Rice could have left because a full-time salary was not available.
11. *MWS*, pp. 38, 45.
12. *MWS*, p. 61.
13. Note to the resume of proceedings before the Supreme Court, 13 Wallace, 687–738, asserts it was Avery, not Hackney, on the session at the time.
14. *MWS*, p. 58.
15. *MWS*, pp. 61–68.
16. *MWS*, p. 63.

17. *MWS*, p. 73.
18. *MWS*, p. 88.
19. *MWS*, p. 85.
20. *MWS*, p. 116.
21. *MWS*, p. 104.
22. *MWS*, pp. 102–118.
23. *MWS*, pp. 134–143.
24. 13 Wallace, 689.
25. Samuel M. Wilson, *History of Kentucky* (Chicago: Clarke Publishing, 1928), 2: 486. Her book was entitled "Poems by Two Sisters of the West."
26. 13 Wallace, 695. It was Justice Harlan, originally from Boyle County, Kentucky, who gave the famous dissent in Plessy v. Ferguson.
27. My article with James C. Hickey, "Implied Trust for Connectional Churches: Watson vs. Jones Revisited," *Journal of Presbyterian History* 54 (1976): 459–470, follows the court cases in more detail and makes an assessment of the doctrine and opinions.
28. Sanders, *Presbyterianism in Paris . . .*, pp. 34, 61, 85.
29. Sanders, *Annals of the First Presbyterian . . .*, pp. 50, 79.
30. Warren, *The Presbyterian Church in Louisville*, pp. 20, 21.
31. Ibid., p. 22.
32. McChord died soon after his election. Finley served for less than a year. The Reverend David Proctor was President *pro tempore*, 1826–27; Gideon Blackburn served as Acting President, 1827–30. See Hardin Craig, *Centre College of Kentucky* (Louisville: Centre College, 1967), p. 10.
33. James H. Hewlett, "Centre College of Kentucky, 1819–1830," *Filson Club History Quarterly* 18 (1944): 178–183. The Presbyterians paid the equivalent of $20,000 in the arrangement, and they began selecting some trustees in 1825.
34. *Minutes*, Synod of Kentucky, 1824, p. 93.
35. Walter Groves, "A School of the Prophets at Danville," *Filson Club History Quarterly* 27 (1953): 223–241. Hewlett, "Centre College . . ." offers detailed information on the School for the Deaf. John A. Jacobs served as its principal from 1825–1869. After his son assumed leadership, the Board of Directors of Centre ceased governing the separate school.
36. Craig, *Centre College . . .*, pp. 14, 15, points out that the bias of Presbyterians in favor of a classical curriculum helped draw the sons of "gentle families" not especially tied to the denomination.
37. John C. Young, born in Greencastle, Pennsylvania, August 12, 1803, died

in Danville June 23, 1857. He married Francis A. Breckinridge, 1829, and then after her death in 1837 married Cornelia Crittenden in 1839. See "A Biographical Sketch of the Rev. John C. Young" in *The Danville Quarterly Review* 4 (1864): 152–166.

38. *Minutes*, General Assembly (Old School) (1853), pp. 121–124.
39. Also named the Danville Henderson Female Institute, it was renamed Caldwell Institute in 1861 and "Kentucky College for Women" in 1913, before the distinct entity became an integral portion of a coeducational Centre College. See Norman L. Snider, "Centre College and the Presbyterians: Cooperation and Partnership," *Register of the Kentucky State Historical Society* 67 (1969): 11.
40. The crucial case involving Centre and Danville was William B. Kincaid et al. v. J. L. McKee, et al. rendered for McKee in the State Court of Appeals, 23 May 1873.
41. Craig, *Centre College . . .*, pp. 34–36.
42. Beatty, an elder in the Danville church, served on several committees of the Old School Assembly. See Walter Groves, "Centre College—The Second Phase, 1830–1857," *Filson Club History Quarterly* 24 (1950): 324.
43. Robert Stuart Sanders, *History of the Louisville Presbyterian Theological Seminary, 1853–1953* (Louisville: Presbyterian Seminary, 1953), pp. 18, 19.

Chapter 7. Into Heartland Presbyterianism

1. Hambleton Tapp and James C. Klotter, *Kentucky: Decades of Discord, 1865–1900* (Frankfort: Kentucky Historical Society, 1977).
2. Robert W. Lynn and Elliott Wright, *The Big Little School: 200 Years of the Sunday School* (1971; reprinted, Birmingham: Religious Education Press, 1980) provides an intimate glimpse of the "resurrection" process. Data from local congregations bears out the autonomy and the later ecumenism in the institutions.
3. *Minutes*, Session, 11 October 1919, p. 239; 6 December 1921, etc. Several congregations, including Second, Louisville, fought at length over the change. Other changes evidently occurred earlier, according to those minutes.
4. *MSK* (PCUS) (1881): 39, 40.
5. For an overall view of the Sunday school plan see E. Morris Fergusson, *Historic Chapters in Christian Education in America* (New York: Fleming H. Revell, 1935).
6. Lucy McGowan, *History of Crescent Hill Presbyterian Church* (Louisville: 1940), pp. 16, 17.

7. *History of Kentucky* (Chicago: S. J. Clarke, 1928), 4: 495.
8. Helm Bruce, *A Savior: Christ the Lord: Bible Studies with the Men's Bible Class of the Second Presbyterian Church* (Louisville: J. P. Morton, 1931), pp. 5 ff. See also *The Patriarch, the Judges, and the Kings* (Louisville: Morton, 1929) and *The Prophets of Israel* (Louisville: Morton, 1930) for further examples.
9. Marion Lawrence, "The Akron Plan—Its Genesis, History and Development," Thirty-Second Annual Report of the Board of Church Extension of the Methodist Episcopal Church, South (1914).
10. *Organized Sunday-School Work in America, 1905–1908* (Chicago: Executive Committee of the International Sunday-School Association, 1908), pp. IX, 19–107.
11. Wilson, *First . . . Maysville*, p. 72, Myers, *First . . . Ashland*, pp. 50, 51. The mention of female officers at Ashland indicates that young women moved immediately into positions of responsibility in the movement.
12. "Tribute to Mrs. Mary G. Skillman," in *Church History of Second Presbyterian Church*, Women of the Church, 1953, available at Montreat, N.C. The Vacation Bible School at Second soon expanded to offer Bible study one afternoon each week during the rest of the year.
13. "Report of Louisville Daily Vacation Bible School Association, 1920." Pamphlet available at Second Presbyterian Church, Louisville. Mrs. Skillman also chaired that association.
14. *MSK*, (PCUS), advised "care" in the process.
15. *Minutes*, Deacons, Second Louisville Presbyterian, February 1887, p. 34.
16. Fergusson, *Historic Chapters . . .*, pp. 186–191.
17. *MGA* (1815, bound with 1789–1820): 594.
18. "Kentucky Synodical Society," a typescript produced by the Board of National Ministries, PCUSA, n.d., p. 1.
19. Ibid, p. 2. This Synodical evidently was the last to be formed in the PCUSA. See Florence Hayes, *Daughters of Dorcas* (New York: Board of National Ministries, PCUSA, 1952), p. 104. The event occurred seven years after organization of the Women's Executive Committee on Home Missions formed to provide a direct channel for women's interests in mission.
20. "Kentucky Synodical . . . ," pp. 2, 3.
21. Mary D. Irvine, with Alice Eastwood, *Pioneer Women of the Presbyterian Church, United States* (Richmond: Presbyterian Committee of Publication, 1923), p. 179.
22. Ibid., pp. 171–184.

23. Ibid. At a denominational level, a measure of the male resistance can be demonstrated in the fact that for a number of years, until hot debate, the Assembly decided to allow only men to read the report from the Woman's Auxiliary on the floor of the Court. See Thompson, *Presbyterians* . . . , III: 401.
24. Irvine, *Pioneer Women* . . . , pp. 178, 179.
25. Elizabeth H. Verdesi, *In But Still Out* (Philadelphia: Westminster, 1973, 1976), pp. 55–78.
26. McGowan, *Crescent Hill* . . . , pp. 28–39, lists some of the projects she presented to her home congregation and undertaken by them.
27. *MSK* (PCUS) (1921): 26, 27. That year the index simply listed "societies," but in 1922 it named "women's societies."
28. *MSK* (PCUS) (1923): 47, 48. See also "Fifty Years of Kentucky Synodical Women of the Church," (n.p.; n.d.) in Historical Foundation, Montreat, N.C.
29. *Christian Observer*, 4 September 1908, p. 899. They gathered especially those of like mind, not necessarily Presbyterian, who were alumni of Centre.
30. The School was first situated at Anchorage, then Bardstown and Paris were considered. Richmond was finally chosen, in part, because townspeople proved especially generous when an initial financial campaign took place. See Jonathan T. Dorris, "Central University, Richmond, Kentucky," a pamphlet in the Presbyterian Historical Foundation, Montreat, N.C., pp. 2–8.
31. The first building was a four-story, central structure, and dormitories were not added until 1883. Dorris, "Central University . . . ," pp. 17–19.
32. Ibid., p. 21. Also, incorporates notes from the file "Central Presbyterian University, Richmond, Kentucky," in the Presbyterian Historical Foundation.
33. Ibid., p. 22; *MSK* (PCUS) (1892): 445, 446.
34. *The Central News*, 23 June 1900, p. 1.
35. Sanders, *Presbyterianism in Paris* . . . , p. 107.
36. Sanders, *History* . . . *Seminary*, pp. 33–44.
37. As Dorris explains, "Central University . . . " (p. 25), pressure on private institutions increased as the public University of Kentucky expanded its offerings. The tasks of educating people grew more complex as disciplines and specialties also increased.
38. Warren, *Presbyterian Church in Louisville*, p. 31.
39. *MSK*, (USA) (1894): 35.

40. Myers, *First . . . Ashland*, pp. 22–34.
41. Fackler, *Chronicle . . .*, pp. 69–75.
42. Unpublished paper by James Watson, Louisville Presbyterian Seminary, 1980; newspaper clippings without mastheads, 24 August 1944.
43. James F. Findlay, Jr., *Dwight L. Moody: American Evangelist, 1837–1899* (Chicago: University Press, 1969), pp. 209, 280. Findlay noted that black people were allotted a small, segregated section. When they asked for more space, Moody promised to return to Louisville to lead a crusade for black people only. He notes that black leaders responded in cool fashion to the offer, and nothing came of it.
44. *Christian Observer*, 18 January 1888, p. 4. Sankey did not arrive until the third week, and a Prof. Case led the choir until then.
45. Ibid., pp. 5, 6. The column also invited ministers coming by rail to apply for passes from the Louisville and Nashville Railroad.
46. *Christian Observer*, 1 February 1888, p. 5. This column also reported the "first fruits" of the effort—23 at First, 14 at Second and unspecified numbers for Highland and Westminster.
47. Scott, *Ministerial Directory . . .*, p. 637. Scudder also served a long pastorate, 40 years in Carlisle and perhaps as many as 52 at Elizaville (most concurrently).
48. Ibid., p. 722.
49. Ibid., p. 458. McDonald was at Henderson, Second Presbyterian at the time.
50. *Christian Observer*, 15 February 1888, p. 5.
51. *Christian Observer*, 29 February 1888, p. 5; *Christian Observer*, 7 March 1888, p. 5.
52. *Christian Observer*, 14 December 1887, p. 5.
53. Sanders, *Annals . . .*, pp. 54, 55.
54. Scott, *Ministerial Directory . . .*, p. 709.
55. Minutes of the Session, Second Presbyterian Church, Lexington, compiled in Sanders, *History . . . Seminary*, p. 144. On Mills, see Thompson, *Presbyterians . . .*, III: 40.
56. Ibid, p. 150. On Smith, see *Gipsy Smith: His Life and Work, by Himself* (New York: Fleming H. Revell, 1902).
57. The "externalization" of revivalism and its movement into the cities remain good topics for exploration. See Martin Marty, *Righteous Empire* (New York: Dial Press, 1970), pp. 162–181.
58. Warren, *Presbyterian Church in Louisville*, p. 27.

59. *Christian Observer*, 2 June 1886, p. 10.
60. *Christian Observer*, 4 January 1888, p. 5.

Chapter 8. Into All Kentucky

1. Thomas H. Spence, *Survey of Records and Minutes in the Historical Foundation of the Presbyterian and Reformed Churches* (Montreat: Historical Foundation Publications, 1943), p. 17.
2. *MSK* (PCUS) (1877), quoted in E. O. Guerrant, *The Soul Winner* (Lexington: J. B. Morton, 1896), p. 121.
3. Robinson had supported E. O. Guerrant in the Synod Committee. On his life, see my "Stuart Robinson: Kentucky Presbyterian Leader," *Filson Club History Quarterly* 54 (1980): 360–377.
4. Thompson, *Presbyterians . . .*, II: 291–293.
5. J. Gray McAllister and Grace Owings Guerrant, *Edward O. Guerrant: Apostle to the Southern Highlands* (Richmond: Richmond Press, 1950), pp. 1–54.
6. Ibid., pp. 55–63; Scott, *Ministerial Directory . . .*, p. 275.
7. McAllister, *Guerrant . . .*, pp. 64–73. In the *Christian Observer*, Dr. W. F. Bishop, who completed his ministry in Louisville, spoke of Guerrant's independent attitudes in seminary. As a student, Guerrant challenged Dabney fiercely on the issue of "whether life insurance is moral." (McAllister, p. 71.)
8. Ibid., pp. 74–89. Forty-three persons were added in his months at the three churches, several score at Mt. Sterling, and in three years the number of members tripled at First Church, Louisville, from about 200 to about 600. *Minutes*, PCUS (1878–1881). On the church itself, see *The First Presbyterian Church of Mt. Sterling, Kentucky* (n.p.: 1955), available at Louisville Presbyterian Theological Seminary.
9. Guerrant, *Soul Winner*, pp. 130–183.
10. This data comes from his report. Notice the variety in locales and congregations.
11. W. O. Shewmaker, from Boyle County, served pastorates in Jackson, Georgetown, and Mt. Pisgah before moving to Connecticut in 1912. He later served as a Bible professor at Southwestern, 1925–41. See McAllister, *Guerrant . . .*, p. 92.
12. E. O. Guerrant, *The Gospel of the Lilies* (Boston: Sherman, French and Co., 1912), for just three of the sermon titles.
13. Ibid., P. 89, in "The Man Born Blind."
14. McAllister, *Guerrant . . .*, pp. 102–120.

15. E.O. Guerrant, *The Galax Gatherers: The Gospel Among the Highlanders*, ed. Grace Guerrant, (Richmond: Onward, 1910), Appendix.
16. McAllister, *Guerrant* . . . , Chapt. XV, pp. 171–180.
17. In *Soul Winner*, p. 251, Guerrant summarized the results of one service:

    The result of the service today was twenty-seven confessions of Christ; thirteen united with the Presbyterian church, eight with the Methodist, and six with the Baptist. Brother Shewmaker baptized the Presbyterians; I baptized the Methodists, at Brother Mann's request, as he was not ordained, and I recommended the Baptist brethren to their own preachers. Most of these people are hereditary Baptists and are tenacious of their inheritance, but their ideas of baptism sometimes need reformation. Aunt Ferraby Noble had to be immersed twice, because she said the water in Leatherwood Creek was not deep enough, so she had it done over and better in Troublesome.
18. McAllister, *Guerrant* . . . , pp. 142, 143.
19. Ibid., pp. 145–149. See also G. Gordon Mahy, *Murdoch of Buckhorn* (Nashville, Tenn.: Parthenon Press, 1946)
20. McAllister, *Guerrant* . . . , pp. 153–157.
21. Egbert W. Smith, "Introduction," *Gospel of the Lilies*, pp. I–VII.
22. Morton, originally from Virginia, later helped as an evangelist for the Synods of North Carolina (1889–91) and Mississippi (1896–99), as other judicatories followed the Kentucky model. Scott, *Ministerial Directory* . . . , p. 523.
23. Ibid., p. 213. He had been the only graduate of Danville Seminary in 1865, and he had served as a presbytery evangelist for several years before his appointment.
24. *MSK* (PCUS) (1884): 132.
25. *Christian Observer* 24 March, 5 April, 28 April, 12 May, 26 May, 1886 (all on p. 5) and 13 May, 1885, p. 4.
26. The collection for each year exceeded $10,000.
27. *MSK* (PCUS) (1893): 504.
28. *Christian Observer* 8 June, 1887, p. 5.
29. *Ibid.*, 23 November, p. 5.
30. *MSK* (PCUS) (1886): 197. Thompson, *Presbyterians* . . . , II: 292.
31. "History of Pikeville College" (1964), a printed pamphlet made available from the school, pp. 5–11.
32. Ibid., p. 10. Early gifts were noted especially from Blythe himself, from the Ashland Church, and from Warren Memorial and College Street churches in Louisville.

33. W. T. Price, *Without Scrip or Purse: The Mountain Evangelist George O. Barnes* (Louisville: W. T. Price, 1883).
34. *Christian Observer*, 27 June, 1888, p. 4.
35. Dickey, who pastored a church in nearby Taylorsville after graduation, later moved to New York and became a Methodist. Pillars later held pastorates in Missouri and Arkansas; he spent several years as a Baptist. Mosely served churches in Texas and Oklahoma. McDowell, a native Kentuckian, returned to pastor the Pisgah Church, 1925–1938. D. D. Little, from Mississippi, was from 1906–1912 a professor in Tuscaloosa, Alabama. John Little, from Alabama, stayed with the work. The variety in background and vocation of the participants seems notable. Scott, *Ministerial Directory*. . . .
36. John Little, "History Notes of the Presbyterian Colored Missions in Louisville," typescript and manuscript in the Archives, University of Louisville. *Christian Observer*, 25 December, 1906, p. 9.
37. Little received remuneration for his work at another mission, for white children. Little, "History Notes . . . ," I:2.
38. *Christian Observer*, 25 December, 1901, p. 9.
39. Little, IV: 1–4.
40. Ibid., II: 10.
41. Ibid., VI: 4.
42. Ibid., V: 1–5.
43. *Minutes*, Presbytery of Louisville, October 12, 1928, p. 12. A memorial noted that "under his leadership it has become an effective church with a roll of 270 members." At Sheppard's funeral white and black pastors made addresses together.
44. Little, "History Notes . . . , " V: 2–3.
45. Louisa M. Woosley, *Shall Woman Preach? or the Question Answered* (Caneyville: n.p., 1891), pp. 189, 190.
46. Ibid., pp. 191, 192.
47. Ibid., p. 195.
48. Ibid. The book named instances all over the world in which women had been received for educational and professional opportunities—in the Moody Institute, in the Campbell Medical School of Calcutta, and in the fields of astronomy, health inspection, and linguistics. "We will now take the boldness of Deborah," she asserted. "Thousands of women are on the stage of action, and they rank, morally and intellectually, with our best and noblest men," pp. 182–184.
49. Barrus, et al., *A People* . . . , pp. 280, 321.

50. Ibid., pp. 321, 429. I cannot determine the relationships of Louisa Woosley and Vianna Woosley from evidence at hand.
51. Mrs. P. L. Clagett, also from Nolin Presbytery, was the first elder seated at a General Assembly in 1893. Barrus, *A People . . .*, p. 280. Their policy became an inclusive one in 1921. Female ruling elders were permitted in the PCUSA in 1930 and in the PCUS in 1964.

Chapter 9. Toward Union

1. William H. Roberts, "The Reunion of the Cumberland Presbyterian Church with the Presbyterian Church in the U.S.A.," *Journal of the Presbyterian Historical Society,* III (Sept. 1906): 301–306.
2. *Minutes,* General Assembly PCUSA, (1903): 38, 242. Roberts makes the point that this revision "was purely a movement within that denomination, and was not at first directly connected in any manner with the Reunion movement." Ibid., p. 302.
3. The CPC initially called its committee a "Committee on Fraternity and Union."
4. Roberts, "The Reunion . . . ," pp. 305, 306. The provision for segregated presbyteries led most black PCUSA leaders to oppose the merger. For the entire "Plan of Reunion," see *The Cumberland Presbyterian* (1904), p. 235.
5. Hubert W. Morrow, "The Background and Development of Cumberland Presbyterian Theology," (Ph.D. dissertation, Vanderbilt University, 1965). A portion of his findings can be located in Barrus, et al., *A People . . .*, Chapter 19, "Progressive Theology."
6. John T. Ames, "Cumberland Liberals and the Reunion of 1906," *Journal of Presbyterian History,* Vol. 52 (1974): 3–18.
7. John Ames has graciously provided for the author his data upon which the published estimates were based. Those figures show 4,043 Cumberland Presbyterians joined the PCUSA.
8. *Minutes,* PCUSA, (1905), pp. 523–525, and (1907), pp. 613–620, show 73 churches in 1905, 188 in 1907. But many congregations were carried on both rolls (CPC and PCUSA) for several years. Perhaps the more illuminating figure is the number of churches in 1910—150.
9. *Minutes,* General Assembly (PCUSA) 1910, pp. 588–594. See also "Columbia — Union Presbyterian Church, 1803 — 1956," a pamphlet available at the Louisville Presbyterian Theological Seminary Library, p. 9.
10. *Minutes,* General Assembly (PCUSA) 1910, pp. 588–594. In places such as Hopkinsville, one Presbyterian congregation was named the "Second Church." See also clipping, February 2, 1905, copied from Trinity University collection (Vol. 69:1–261) in materials collected by F. C. Pogue and

provided for inspection and use in this volume.

11. *Minutes,* General Assembly (PCUSA) 1910, p. 589.
12. The Lincoln Presbytery was re-integrated into geographical component presbyteries in 1934.
13. "Agreements for Consolidation of the Presbyterian Theological Seminaries at Danville and Louisville under the name of Presbyterian Theological Seminary of Kentucky, and of Centre College and Central University, under the name of Central University of Kentucky," second edition (1901), pp. 1–19. Available in the Presbyterian Historical Foundation, Montreat, N.C.
14. Sanders, *History of Louisville Presbyterian Theological Seminary,* p. 45.
15. *Catalogue, Central University of Kentucky, Danville (1901–2, 1902–3)* available in Archives, Centre College.
16. Craig, *Centre College . . . ,* pp. 55, 56. This assertion was balanced by the claim that PCUS dominance was recognized at the Louisville Seminary. Confirmed in interview with Dr. Cheek, September 1981.
17. Craig, *Centre College . . . ,* pp. 62–70.
18. Sanders, *History of Louisville Presbyterian Theological Seminary,* pp. 45–56.
19. Ibid., p. 54.
20. "Plan of Union" between the UPCUSA and the PCUS is to be considered which would make all ten seminaries of the combined church like Louisville Presbyterian Theological Seminary in this respect.
21. Carrie D. Marshall, *Sixty-Six Years at the Same Corner: Highland Presbyterian Church* (n.p.: 1942). Available at church.
22. *First Presbyterian Church of Mt. Sterling . . . ,* p. 63.
23. Sanders, *Presbyterianism in Paris . . . ,* pp. 76–79.
24. "Service of Formal Consummation of Union, May 11, 1913, United Presbyterian Church, Harrodsburg, Kentucky." (Printed bulletin, available in the Louisville Presbyterian Seminary Library.) pp. 2, 3.
25. *Presbyterian Survey* 45 (1955): 20–22, 34.
26. Interview with officers in the Harrodsburg Presbyterian Church, 8 November, 1981.
27. Thompson, *Presbyterians . . . ,* III: 572, 573.
28. *Southern Presbyterian Journal,* 9 February 1955, p. 14.
29. "History of Harvey Browne Presbyterian Church," 2 vols., typescript in local Church History section, Historical Foundation, Montreat, N.C. Interviews with Olof Anderson, May 1982.

30. Louis Weeks, "Second Presbyterian Church, Louisville: A Local Church History," in press, 1983. Chapters IV–VII.
31. Ibid., Chapter VI.
32. *Minutes,* Fourth Avenue Presbyterian Church, Louisville, Ky., XIII: 193. Available in Louisville Presbyterian Theological Seminary Library.
33. *Of Our Own Household: Tasks of the Presbyterians in Kentucky* (Synod of Kentucky, PCUS: 1927), pp. 91–96.
34. Interview with the Superintendent of Bellewood, Elder Robert Hawks, Anchorage Presbyterian Church, 15 November 1981.
35. Louisville *Courier–Journal,* 27 November 1957, Section 3, p. 1. "The Bulletin," Women's Club of Louisville, December 1962, pp. 2–7; and other materials provided by Mrs. John Green.
36. *Of Our Own Household,* p. 35.
37. Edwin W. Stock, Jr., "The Role of the Church in the Inception and Survival of the Appalachian Regional Hospitals," unpublished D. Min. dissertation, Louisville Presbyterian Seminary, 1979, pp. 1–53.
38. Ibid., pp. 90–95.

INDEX